CARD
WEAVING

CARD WEAVING

BY CANDACE CROCKETT

ILLUSTRATIONS BY LAWRENCE DUKE

WATSON-GUPTILL PUBLICATIONS, NEW YORK

PITMAN PUBLISHING, LONDON

"For Kent and Christopher"

Copyright © 1973 by Watson-Guptill Publications
First published 1973 in the United States and Canada by Watson-Guptill Publications,
a division of Billboard Publications, Inc.
One Astor Plaza, New York, N.Y. 10036

Published simultaneously in Great Britain by Sir Isaac Pitman & Sons Ltd.,
39 Parker Street, Kingsway, London WC2B 5PB
ISBN 0-273-00415-8

Manufactured in U.S.A.

Library of Congress Cataloging in Publication Data
Crockett, Candace, 1945–
  Card weaving.
  1. Card weaving. I. Title.
TT848.C67 1973   746.1'4   73-6913
ISBN 0-8230-0562-3

First Printing, 1973
Second Printing, 1974

ACKNOWLEDGMENTS

I am most grateful to the following institutions for making their collections available for research and reproduction: the Collection of Antiquities, Oslo University; the Liverpool Museum; the Museum of Ethnology and Prehistory, Hamburg; the National Museum, Copenhagen; the Smithsonian Institution, Washington, D.C.; the Victoria and Albert Museum, London.

I would also especially like to thank the following people for generously contributing their work and their time: Bettie Adams, Joyce Arata, Marie Arejula, Donna Armstrong, Marie Backs, Julia Bauder, Janet Becklund, Anne Blinks, Susan Boblitt, Liz Brierley, Vera Brown, Janet Bucknam, Patricia Campbell, Roxanne Clarke, Irene Conley, Robert Cranford, Lawrence Duke, Jack Dunstan, Helene Durbin, Lillian Elliott, Linda Griggs, Ana Lisa Hedstrom, Lorraine Herald, Toni Horgos, Judy Kinnell, Carol Krieg, Dolores Levin, Gail Manners, Ricardo Mata, Phoebe McAfee, Flora Milligan, Diana Mitchell, Karen Myers, Bob Nugent (photographer), Hilda Rasmussen, Linda Scofield, Kay Sekimachi, Lynda Sexauer, Stone and Stecati (photographers), Kenneth Storey, Joyce Wexler, Jacquie Wilson, Jackie Wollenberg, Nancy Woodward.

CONTENTS

1. A HISTORY OF CARD WEAVING

Figure 1. A 16th century French tapestry in Rheims Cathedral, showing a card weaving with six-holed tablets strung between two columns. Courtesy of the Victoria and Albert Museum, London.

Card weaving is an ancient craft in which simple, flat tablets, or cards, form the "loom" structure (see Figure 2). Although it requires little equipment and is easy to learn, card weaving is a sophisticated craft capable of producing a weave unavailable with any other technique. The simplicity and the relative ease of working with the cards, the complexity and variety of patterns, the full texture and beauty of the woven fabric, and even its rich history all make card weaving a uniquely rewarding and gratifying activity.

Card Weaving: An Explanation

In loom weaving the longitudinal threads, or warp, pass through "harnesses" that allow the weaver to form a "shed," or space, through which he passes the weft thread. In card weaving, the shed is created by turning or rotating the cards, usually as a unit. The cards themselves can be of just about any shape or size, but most are square, about $4'' \times 4''$, with a hole in each corner. Once the cards are threaded, with the warp threads passed through the card holes and anchored for tension at each end, the "loom" is ready (this process is described in detail in Chapter 3).

Card weaving is a warp-face technique. The threads that are visible in the completed weaving are the warp—longitudinal threads that were originally threaded through the card holes. The weft thread acts to bind the warp threads in place and is hidden in the weaving. Each rotation, or turn of the cards, brings new warp threads to the surface, forming a new shed through which the weft thread will pass. The four threads that go through the holes in each card twist as the cards are rotated, so if four-holed cards are used, the result is a four-ply fabric. This spiraling, or twisting, of the warp threads is characteristic of—and unique to—card weaving. It forms an

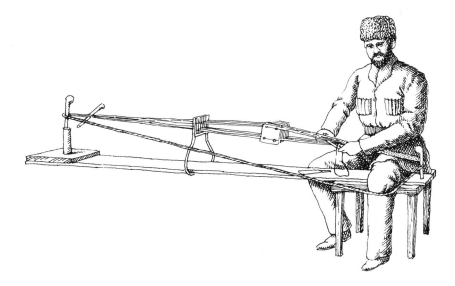

Figure 2. A Caucasian tablet weaver from Kutais, Georgia (U.S.S.R.), after a sketch done originally by M. Bartels in 1897. The weaver is working on a circular warp, and as the weaving progresses he moves the warp around. Tension is maintained by the pegs and the weaver's knee.

important structural element of the craft, relating it directly to braiding and cordmaking (just as the use of the weft thread relates it to loom weaving). The direction of the twist in the warp threads, to the right or to the left, is determined by the way the cards are turned and by how individual cards are threaded.

Much of the unique beauty of card weaving is the result of these twists in the warp-face of the fabric. In order to avoid tangling the unwoven warp threads, the weaver periodically reverses the direction of the turning of the cards. This changes the angle of the twist and also changes the overall design of the weaving by creating reversals.

Patterns in Card Weaving

Card weaving offers unique richness of texture and variety of pattern. Simply by shifting the positions of individual cards—or groups of cards—laterally, the weaver can create new textures and new patterns. Complex patterns can easily be predetermined by plotting them on a simple grid, as explained in Chapters 4 and 5. The modern card weaver can create his own designs, or he can use traditional patterns that were first woven hundreds or even thousands of years ago. Once the pattern is determined and the cards are threaded, the weaving goes very quickly, but the weaver can change or expand upon the pattern he has chosen at any time. Many card weavers get special pleasure from the knowledge of the creative potential in each turn of the cards.

The Origins and Distribution of Card Weaving

Evidence of early sophistication in card weaving has been found in North Africa, Egypt, Europe, Asia, and Iceland. Ancient card weavings have been found in Egypt and Scandinavia, but it's impossible to say where or by whom card weaving was invented. There are strong indications that it has a long and varied history in Russia and in China. It's quite possible that card weaving was in use many thousands of years before the Christian Era, and that it was brought from Egypt through Rome to western and northern Europe. The oldest known card weavings come from Egypt. Scandinavian finds are not as old but are far richer. Whether from Egypt, Scandinavia, or the East, card weaving spread throughout Europe and was in wide popular use through the sixteenth century.

Traditional Tools and Materials

The techniques, colors, patterns, materials, and cards differ from one geographical area to the next, depending on available materials and on tradition. Cards have been found made of stone, wood, bone, horn, tortoise shell, ivory, fish skin, parchment, leather, and even of playing cards trimmed and punched for use in weaving. The size, number, and placement of holes, as well as the shape of the cards, varies. The materials used to weave with

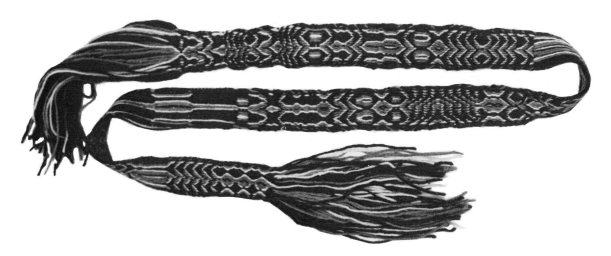

Figure 3. A sampler made with acrylic yarn, 2″ wide. The sampler shows pattern variations achieved by turning the cards as a unit in different sequences. More pattern variation can be achieved by turning individual cards.

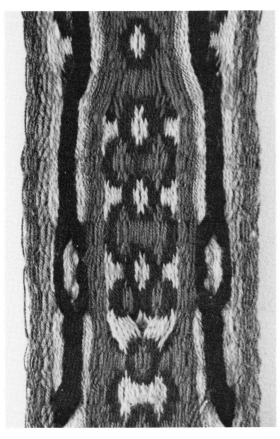

Figure 4. Detail of a wall hanging made with wool yarn, 7½″ wide, by Helene Durbin. The pattern is broken and changed by moving groups of cards laterally during the weaving process.

Figure 5. Detail of a wall hanging made of wool with copper wire, 11″ wide, by Dolores Levin. This detail shows the results of shifting tension in parts of the weaving to create dimension and texture (see Chapter 7). In some areas the warp becomes the weft.

range from coarse handspun wool and hair yarns to linen, silk, and spun gold. Fine wool and cotton threads have always been widely used. Brocading was done using gold and silver threads, and in some cases human hair.

Card weaving began as peasant craft, but became a highly sophisticated court craft as well after about 800 A.D. Many of the old examples, particularly from the Middle Ages, are incredibly intricate. Some used hundreds of cards and fine silk for bands with inscriptions and decorative motifs. Such intricate bands were often woven on cards no more than 2″ square.

Card Weaving in Ancient Egypt

The Egyptians are frequently credited with the invention and development of card weaving. In 1916, van Gennep and Jequier published a beautiful and influential book on card weaving, and presented their argument that it was invented by the Egyptians before the year 4000 B.C. and was highly developed by the year 2000 B.C. Their premises are highly questionable, but if one is willing to accept a number of assumptions, then their argument could be convincing. Their position is dependent upon the recurrence in ancient Egyptian statuary and paintings of designs such as the chevron and the zigzag, which are frequently associated with card weaving (Figure 6). Another factor in van Gennep's argument involved the girdle of Rameses III (Figure 7), an incredible piece of weaving 17 feet long, presently in excellent condition, and firmly dated from near 1200 B.C. Unfortunately it's questionable whether this piece is card woven. None of the characteristics unique to card weaving are present in the weaving, and van Gennep never actually saw or examined the piece, but worked from photographs. At any rate, van Gennep and Jequier presented evidence strong enough to create a controversy that has lasted to the present day (Figure 8). No cards have been found in Egypt dating earlier than the Coptic period (25 wooden, four-holed tablets were found in the Gayet

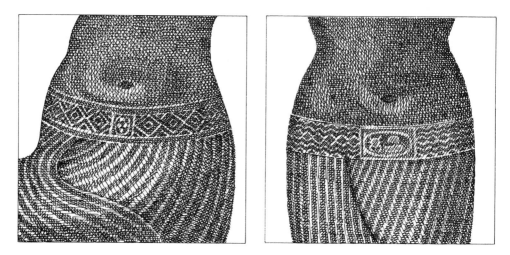

Figure 6. Facsimiles of designs found on Egyptian statuary from the 18th dynasty. Early 20th century scholars felt that such designs on painting and statuary were indications that card weaving existed in ancient Egypt.

Figure 7. *The girdle of Rameses III, 1200 B.C. from Egypt. Blue, red, yellow, green, and natural linen, 17 feet long. The width tapers from 5" to 1⅞" by decreasing warp threads in the center. The number of warp threads varies from 272 to 340 per inch. Experts have agreed on the structure as being double weave, but they haven't agreed on the weaving technique. The indications that it was loom-woven are convincing. Courtesy of the Liverpool Museum.*

Figure 8. *Contemporary wool belt, 3" wide, by Robert Cranford. The ankh design was adapted from the girdle of Rameses III.*

excavations at Antinoe from the fourth and fifth centuries A.D.) Loom implements and drawings of looms from earlier times have been found but not of cards or of card looms. Three narrow linen bands dating from the twenty-second dynasty (945–745 B.C.) are the oldest known card weavings and appear to be from Egypt, but the next card-woven pieces date from the Coptic period hundreds of years later (Figure 9). Considering the wealth of textiles recovered from Egypt, card woven pieces are very few. The pieces found are simple and lack sophistication.

Card Weaving in Scandinavia

In Scandinavia, card weaving can be traced back to the Celtic Bronze Age, beginning in the second century A.D., and to the Iron Age, beginning in the eighth century A.D. Bronze Age card weaving was used as a means for binding and spacing the warp threads on the warp-weighted loom then in common use. These early pieces were card-woven with weft threads that dangled from the strip, so that while the card-woven band was quite narrow, each weft thread was fringelike and just as long as the loom-woven piece was to be. Thus the narrow strip would be stretched across the top of the loom, and what had been weft threads in the card weaving became warp threads on the loom, hanging vertically and held in place with weights (Figures 10 and 11). The finished loom-woven fabric would then have a narrow card-woven band along its upper margin, and would have as warp threads the well-spaced weft threads from the narrow card-woven band. This technique is known to have existed in Norway as early as the third century A.D. These card-woven borders were apparently always an important part of the fabric produced, and not merely a technical means of creating or spacing warp threads. In later Scandinavian loom weavings, card-woven borders, often very intricate, were woven separately and sewn onto the finished textile.

The earliest known cards are two wooden tablets, each with four holes, found in Denmark and dating from the early Iron Age. The greatest treasures, however, came from the Oseberg ship find in Norway, dated around 850 A.D. A tablet loom with fifty-two threaded cards, a partially woven band, and a number of other card-woven bands, some with diagonal patterns and others with brocading, were found at Oseberg. Archeological discoveries from the Viking trading center of Birka in Sweden revealed a number of technically sophisticated card-woven bands from the period 800–975 A.D. Some of the bands are brocaded in gold, others are of pure silk, and some are a combination of linen and silk.

Card Weaving in Medieval Europe

Archeological remains indicate that card weaving was known in western Europe from Roman times. It existed primarily as a peasant craft, using natural, undyed wools. Trade with the East, beginning especially with the ninth century, brought silk, and very probably fine card weavings, to the

Figure 9. *Egyptian band in wool and linen from the 7th-10th century* A.D. *Courtesy of the Victoria and Albert Museum, London.*

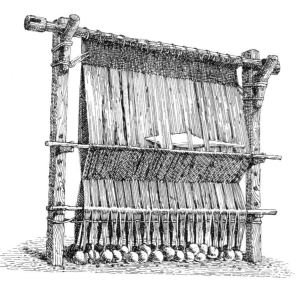

Figure 10. *(Above) A drawing of the warp-weighted loom in use in ancient Scandinavia. A card-woven band across the top of the warp was sometimes used to bind and space the loom warp (Illustration after H. Ling Roth, Ancient and Greek Looms).*

Figure 11. *(Right) A brown wool skirt by Anne Blinks. This is a copy of the Bronze Age Egtved skirt in the Danish Museum, Copenhagen. It was done with two-holed cards in a plain weave. The card-woven band along the top functions in much the same way as it does on the warp-weighted loom. The loose arrangement of twisted threads which make up the skirt are pulled through the card weaving as weft.*

court of Charlemagne and to other European trade and cultural centers. Textiles preserved from the Middle Ages indicate that card weaving rapidly became a highly refined technique of craftsmen, and even of court ladies, who were able to use very fine silk in combination with gold and silver threads. Frequently these pieces were used as trim on church vestments, bands or seals for precious documents, or as trim on court clothing. Bands were sometimes prepared as special gifts commemorating important occasions or events. There's no doubt that card-woven bands were commonly used on less precious garments, very few of which have survived.

A cingulum, or girdle, dedicated to Bishop Witgarius of Augsburg, dated 870 A.D., is the earliest extant card weaving from medieval Europe. This remarkable belt is worked in red silk, with gold brocading, and has a beautiful inscription done in fine Roman capitals. The piece displays refined craftsmanship and superb technical mastery. In England the card-woven bands from the vestments of St. Cuthbert at Durham (916 A.D.) are fine belts of red silk brocaded with gold. One of these bands combines a diagonal weave in the center with a fine plain weave on the borders. It's worked in ways reminiscent of bands woven in Norway in the fifth and sixth centuries. Card weaving survived the Middle Ages in Europe just as it had survived in Asia, but it had passed its period of greatest sophistication, and its "rediscovery" in the late nineteenth century could come only after serious archeological and academic study.

The Rediscovery of Card Weaving

For the Western world, card weaving was rediscovered at the turn of this century by a German scholar, Margarethe Lehmann-Filhes. This rediscovery was sparked by the great surge of interest in archeological studies stimulated by the successes of Schliemann and others during the latter part of the nineteenth century. A bone card weaving tablet found at Birka, Sweden, in 1873 added greatly to the interest, as did studies of card weaving in India in the 1880's. During this time Margarethe Lehmann-Filhes began serious study of Icelandic card weaving. In order to understand the weaving she actually reconstructed the techniques, and for all practical purposes card weaving was rediscovered. She developed plain weave, double-face, and double-weave bands. Her investigations and discoveries opened the door to an understanding of the history and widespread distribution of card weaving, as well as of its technical aspects. Tablets and cards that had long collected dust on museum shelves were suddenly identified as weaving tools. Only then was it realized that card weaving had a full and rich history, and that it was still being practiced in widely separated parts of the world. Her interest led to the publication in 1901 of *Ueber Brettchenweberei*, in which she described and explained card weaving. Popular magazines ran articles, serious literature was published, museums put on special shows, and card weaving collections were established.

Card Weaving in Asia and the Middle East

Card weaving has been an ongoing craft in Asia and the Middle East since its origins. Card weaving came to Burma and the surrounding area of Southeast Asia from China and India and it penetrated to the Himalayan countries from North India. Card weavings are still made for export from these areas. Japanese card weavings are notable for their plain weave and simple patterns, very often in heavy lustrous silk. The most exciting card weavings from China are heavy, stiff, functional bands for saddle girths done in zigzag patterns and woven with six-holed cards. In Burma, card weaving has been closely related to religion, and monks' belts and special bands with religious inscriptions have been produced for centuries. Card weaving has flourished in widely separated parts of the East and Middle East, and bands and belts are even now being woven in several Eastern, Middle Eastern, and North African countries.

Card Weaving Today

Card weaving was introduced into the United States by Mary Meggs Atwater in the 1920's. She and others popularized the craft among American weavers, but only considerably later did weavers such as Lillian Elliott begin to gain attention with tapestries and wall hangings. Card weaving is now enjoying an active revival in the United States. An increasing number of excellent card weavings are to be seen in contemporary American weaving shows and exhibitions, as well as in the more vigorous and exciting craft fairs. The emphasis of interest is no longer on the past perfection of the art; most modern card weavers are attracted by the pleasure of planning and producing beautiful materials, whatever their use. Modern weavers might well choose to reproduce examples first woven hundreds of years ago, but for the most part contemporary card weavings show a fresh approach that can only be applied to a new or recently rediscovered art form. It's especially gratifying to see an ancient art reinterpreted and redefined as energetically and as successfully as card weaving is in the United States today.

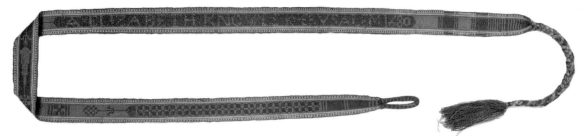

Figure 12. A garter inscribed, "Elizabeth Knowls, Jerusalem, 1680." This is one of many inscribed garters from the Near East that appeared in England during the second half of the 17th century. They are generally card-woven and bear the word "Jerusalem" along with names and dates (although one was found with the word "Smirna," indicating that not all were from Jerusalem). Courtesy of the Victoria and Albert Museum, London.

Figure 13. (Above) A complete loom with 52 wooden tablets found in the tomb of Queen Asa. This is part of the Oseberg ship find from 850 A.D. The partially finished band was found along with other card-woven bands, some with brocaded patterns and diagonal pattern weaves. Courtesy of the Collection of Antiquities, Oslo University.

Figure 14. (Right) The back of a 12th century Islamic card weaving. The green, red, white, and black band is silk with gold brocading, and is presumably Sicilian or German. Courtesy of the Victoria and Albert Museum, London.

Figure 15. The front of a French ecclesiastical card weaving from the 12th century. The warp is silk with gold and silver brocading and gold embroidery. Courtesy of the Victoria and Albert Museum, London.

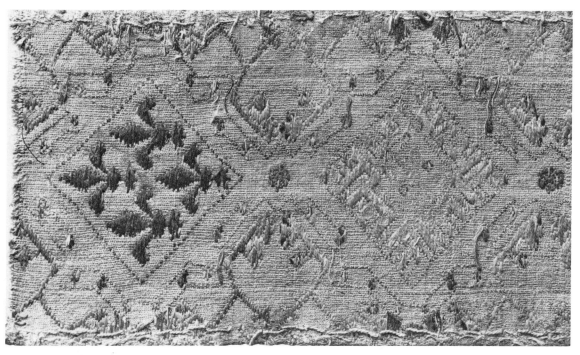

Figure 16. The back of the card weaving shown in Figure 15.

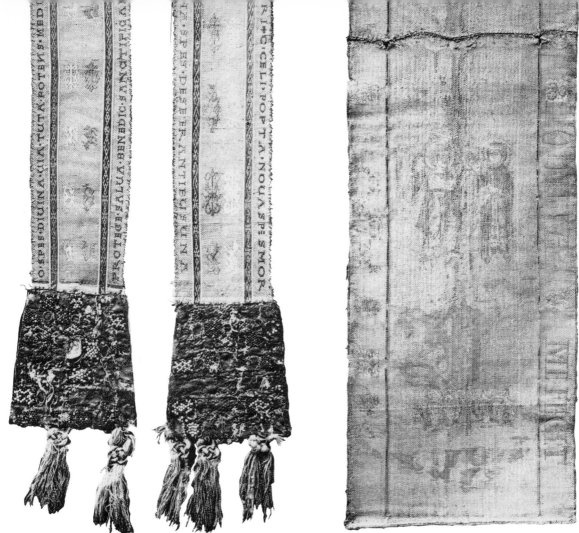

Figure 17. *A maniple (an ornamental band; one of the Eucharistic vestments), probably Sicilian, in silk with gold threads dating from the early 13th century. Courtesy of the Victoria and Albert Museum, London.*

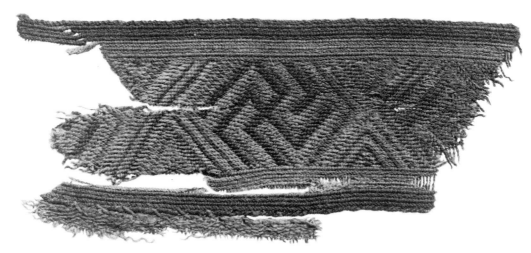

Figure 18. *A section of a 6th century* A.D. *wool band found in a man's grave at Lyngdal, Norway. The patterns were woven in blue, red, and yellow. Courtesy of the Collection of Antiquities, Oslo University.*

Figure 19. *A stole with silk warp, probably Sicilian, dating from the 13th century. The pattern is entirely gold brocading. Courtesy of the Victoria and Albert Museum, London.*

Figure 20. *Two wooden, four-holed tablets from the early Celtic Iron Age. They belong to the cart find from Deibjergbog. Courtesy of the National Museum, Copenhagen.*

Figure 21. (Right) Contemporary handspun wool camel strap in orange, red, blue, and purple, 1½" wide, from the Middle East. Courtesy of Helene Durbin.

Figure 22. (Below) A card weaving loom from Hara S'rira, Djerba Island, Tunisia. The date is uncertain. The cards are suspended in the middle and at each end is a device for winding up the warp. Courtesy of the Museum of Ethnology and Prehistory, Hamburg.

Figure 23. (Left) Section of a contemporary woolen Turkish belt in red, black, purple, and white, 1½″ wide. Beads and fleece were added to the braided fringe. Courtesy of Lillian Elliott.

Figure 24. (Below) A contemporary camel strap in natural wool shades, 1½″ wide, from the Middle East. Courtesy of Anne Blinks.

2. MATERIALS

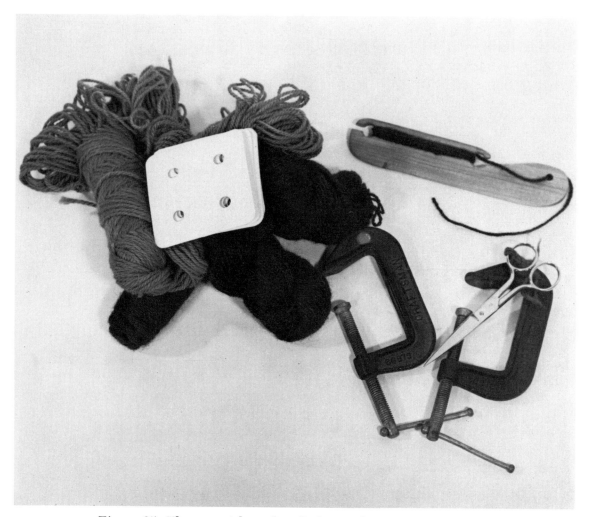

Figure 25. *The materials and tools for card weaving. Yarn, scissors, and four-holed cards are necessities. C-clamps are convenient for wrapping the warp and for anchoring the weaving. A belt shuttle is useful for holding the weft yarn and for beating it into place.*

The tools and equipment needed for card weaving are very simple: cards and yarn. Two C-clamps are handy to measure the warp threads before the cards are threaded, and a small belt shuttle is helpful during the weaving process, but neither is absolutely necessary. (Figure 25).

Cards

Although cards of different shapes and sizes with a varied number of holes can be used, the four-holed square card (Figure 26) is the easiest shape to work with and in most cases gives the best results. A single piece of weaving might use as few as five cards or as many as several hundred. The sample pattern band in Chapter 3 requires 10 cards. The bands discussed in Chapters 4 and 5 require from 10 to 65 cards each. With only a few exceptions the weavings pictured in this book were produced with four-holed square cards. Square cards can be purchased from most weaving stores (see the Suppliers List, p. 140) at minimal cost, or you can make your own using poster board or medium-weight cardboard. The cards shown actual size in Figures 26–28 may be used as patterns.

The cards should be stiff enough to hold their shape, and shouldn't buckle during turning. If the cardboard is too thick, however, the cards become bulky, heavy, and difficult to work with. Card holes can either be drilled or punched. A paper punch makes satisfactory holes although they're not as large as those on the templates. Corners should be slightly rounded so that they don't catch the warp threads as the cards turn. The hole in the center of some manufactured cards is used to carry an extra warp thread, which increases the thickness, stiffness, and strength of the fabric. This center thread, which isn't usually used in contemporary card weaving, is hidden from view, and consequently doesn't alter the pattern. A thin dowel is occasionally placed through the central holes of a pack of cards to keep the cards in order during weaving. Varnish or shellac can be used to strengthen cards, and with unusually heavy or harsh materials weavers sometimes glue two cards together for extra strength.

Generally, the size and weight of the card is determined by the thickness and roughness of the thread. The holes on just one side—the "face" side—of the cards are lettered or numbered. This aids the weaver in threading when a specific pattern is being used. Many weavers prefer to work without a pattern, and in such cases the letters or numbers are ignored. Square cards are most convenient to handle, and they make a large clear weaving shed. Six-holed cards have a greater design potential than four-holed cards, but they're difficult to keep in order and create a very thick fabric. Three-holed triangular cards are also difficult to handle, and don't have the design potential of four-holed cards. The two basic "shed" positions for weaving with four-holed square cards are shown in Figure 29. The diagrams shown in Figures 26–29 will be especially helpful for future reference, and for the weaver who chooses to experiment with three- and six-holed cards. Weaving with four-holed cards is explained fully in Chapter 3.

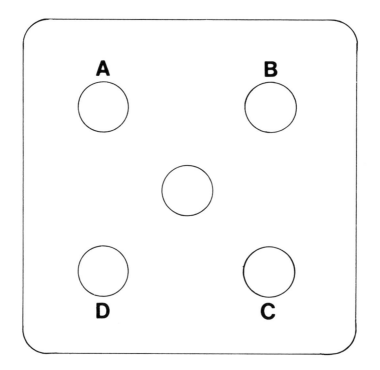

Figure 26. A four-holed square card shown actual size. The hole in the center is rarely used. This is the most popular and functional card for card weaving.

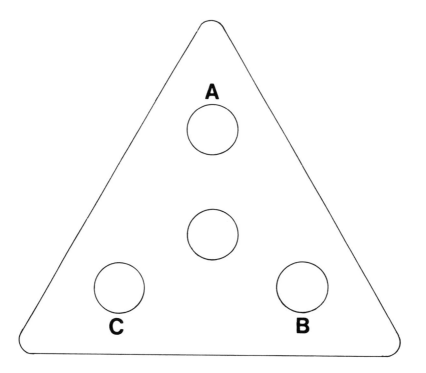

Figure 27. A three-holed triangular card shown actual size.

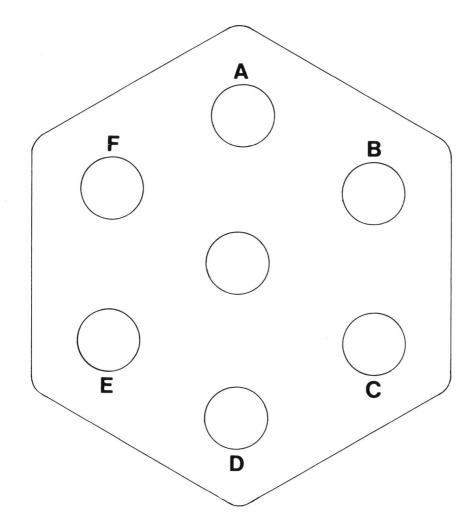

Figure 28. A six-holed hexagonal card shown actual size.

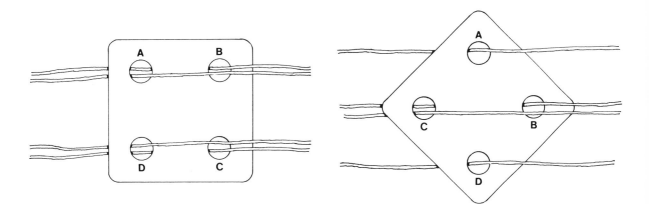

Figure 29. The two basic "shed" positions for four-holed cards. These diagrams show the possible positions of the cards as they are suspended by the warp threads under tension.

Warp Yarns

The warp threads are those that go through the card holes and are anchored at each end to suspended cards on the threads. These warp threads must be quite strong, and smooth enough to allow the cards to move back and forth over them. If the yarn isn't strong the threads will shred and break; if it's not relatively smooth the fuzzy threads will catch and the cards will be difficult to turn. As the weaver gains experience in card weaving he'll be able to work the cards easily with both rough and delicate materials. Some weavers prefer working with mercerized cotton because of its smooth texture, and wool is popular because of its rich colors and springy nature. Most generally available knitting yarns come in vivid colors that are very exciting in card-woven patterns. Knitting wool, however, is often difficult for the beginner because of its stretchiness, but it can be used very successfully by the experienced weaver.

Weaving yarns are generally best for card weaving: they have relatively little stretch and are available in a wide range of quality, color, material, and weight. Handspun yarns can be used, but require great care. Handspun warp threads should be tightly spun or spun in the grease (yarns retaining their natural oils). Loosely spun or lumpy yarn will disintegrate as the cards move and turn. For best results beginners should use only a few cards and a medium-weight plied yarn in wool or cotton. Linen and silk also work up beautifully in card weaving, but should be used only after the process has become familiar. Some of the heavier, more resistant fibers, such as jute and sisal, can be enjoyable to work and experiment with, have great potential for wall hangings, and usually dye well. Synthetic

Figure 30. Fibers for card weaving must be strong and relatively smooth. The beginner should work with a smooth, plied-wool or plied-cotton yarn.

materials such as wire, rope, monofilament, and plastic cord are exciting and dimensional, but require experience and special consideration.

Materials not ordinarily associated with weaving, such as ribbon, leather, and fabric strips, have serious potential in card weaving. Different materials and varying weights of yarn can be combined in one weaving, but since some materials stretch more than others, adjustments may have to be made at the anchor points during the weaving process.

Weft Yarns

Any weaving results from the interlacing of a weft thread with the warp threads. In card weaving, the weft thread goes through the shed formed by each turn of the cards. It pulls the warp threads together and holds them in place. Because card weaving is a warp-face technique, the weft thread will be hidden in the weaving, showing only on the edge where it "goes around the corner." If the weft thread is the same color as the warp threads that go through the outside or border cards, the weft thread won't be noticeable.

Often, and especially when the warp threads are bulky, a lighter weft thread packs down most easily and won't hump along the edges. Sometimes other threads or raw wool may be inserted along with the weft thread to create a fringe on one or both sides. Sticks, rods, bones, feathers, and many other materials may be laid in with the weft thread to add to the texture and color of the weaving.

Shuttles

The weft thread can be wound into a "butterfly" (Figure 31) and carried through the shed quite easily in most weavings. It's then beaten into place with a kitchen knife, ruler, or with bare fingers. Many weavers, however, prefer a small belt shuttle that both holds the weft thread and helps in beating it into place. Any good shuttle will probably be smooth, well rounded, and free of rough spots that might snag the yarn. The shuttle in Figure 30 is 1¾" wide and 8" long. The hole on the shuttle prevents accidental unwinding.

C-Clamps

Since the warp threads in a card weaving are usually all the same length, some means must be found to conveniently measure many warp threads at once.

One widely used method for measuring warp threads is to attach two C-clamps to a bench or table (Figure 45) and then wrap the appropriate number of threads around the securely anchored clamps. This allows for flexibility in determining the length of the warp, and assures uniform tension. These C-clamps may also be used as anchor points for the card weaving as shown in Figure 50.

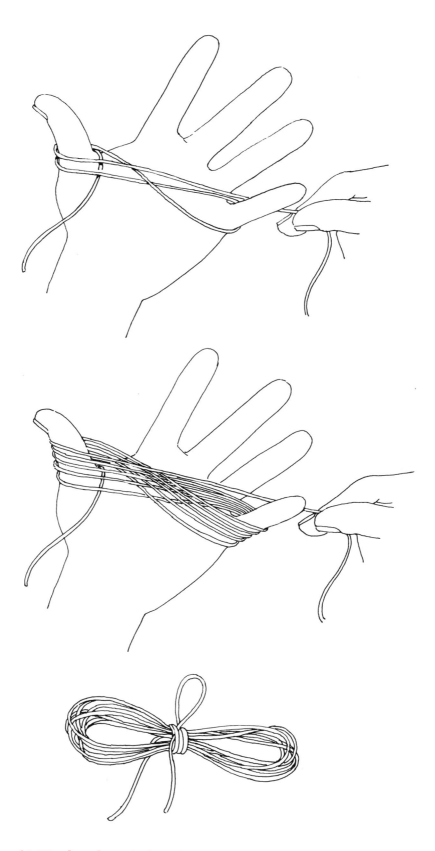

Figure 31. Winding the weft thread into a "butterfly."

Figure 33. Detail of a wall hanging in handspun, single-ply wool, 9″ wide, by Lynda Sexauer.

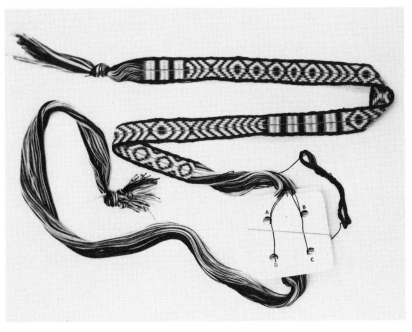

Figure 32. (Left) Mercerized cotton band, 4″ wide, by Patricia Campbell.

Figure 34. (Above) Fine cotton sampler, 1″ wide.

Figure 35. Detail of a wool and copper wire wall hanging by Dolores Levin.

Figure 36. (Right) *Sculpture of plastic coated wire, 13″ x 23″, by Dolores Levin.*

Figure 37. (Left) *A card weaving wrapped with another card weaving, made of plastic raffia and sisal, 2½″ wide. Woven by Lillian Elliott.*

3. TECHNIQUES

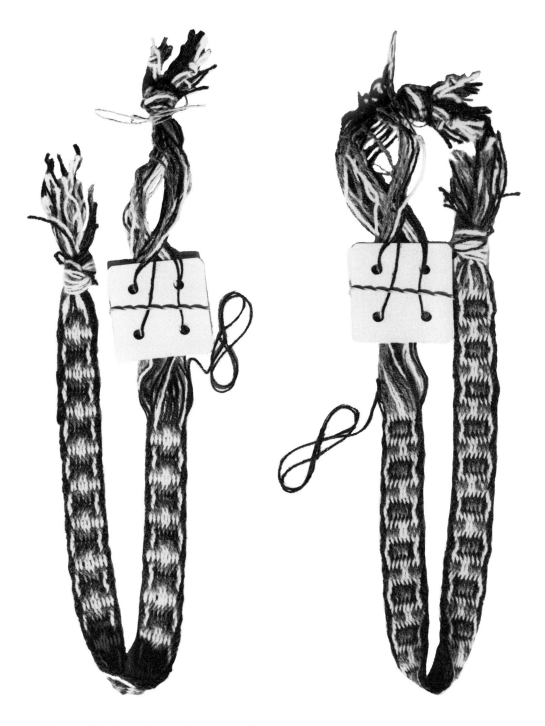

Figure 38. *Sample Band A partially woven, using dark, medium, and light threads as drafted in Figure 41.*

Figure 39. *The back view of Sample Band A.*

The first two chapters of this book acquainted you with the history, appearance, and tools of card weaving. This chapter shows you how to weave a sample belt using a set pattern. It's important to follow the directions for each step very carefully if you're a beginner. Once you've mastered the basic technique of card weaving you'll be shown, in later chapters, how to create your own designs and how to weave in more sophisticated ways. Remember that your first card weaving will be the most difficult one, so give yourself time to work carefully.

If you follow each step in this chapter you'll weave a belt very much like the one in Figures 38 and 39. (Sample Band A). It's a bold and distinct design, and the pattern is particularly easy to follow. The weaving requires just 10 cards, an easily worked number for a beginning card weaver. The band in the photograph used a 3-ply rug yarn.

List of Materials

These are the basic materials you'll need for weaving Sample Band A. The materials for any card weaving will be similar, although the number and type of card, the number of warp strands, and the type of yarn will change.

10 square four-holed cards (lettered A, B, C, and D).

40 warp strands (16 dark, 14 light, 10 medium) each 72″ long.

Dark thread for the weft (about a 2″ ball of yarn).

A rubber band and a shuttle.

The Pattern Draft

Figure 41 is the pattern draft for Sample Band A. It gives all the information necessary for threading the cards. Each of the numbers across the bottom represents an individual card (10 cards are needed). The letters A, B, C, and D, on the left-hand side of the diagram represent the lettered holes in the cards. Each hole in each card will have its own thread, and each of these threads is represented as a square in the pattern draft. The pattern draft shows you what color thread goes through each hole. Card 5, for example, has a medium color threaded through hole A, a dark color threaded through hole B, a light color threaded through hole C, and a light color threaded through hole D.

Threading the Cards

Figures 42 and 43 show the two basic ways of threading cards. The front, or lettered side of the card should always be considered the left-hand side, or the side that will face the weaver's left during weaving. The unlettered side is the back, or right-hand side. The direction of the arrow on the pattern draft tells you from which side to thread each card. An arrow to the right on the diagram means that you thread the card from left to right

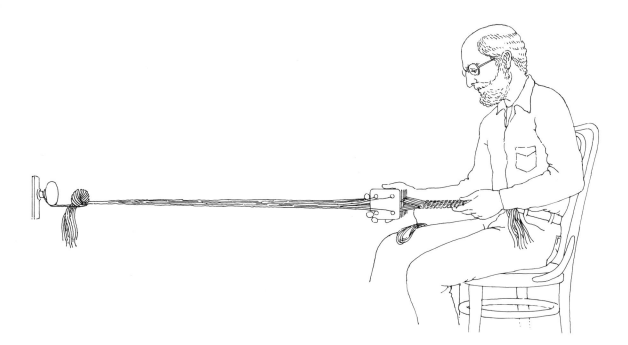

Figure 40. *A card weaving in progress.*

Fig 41

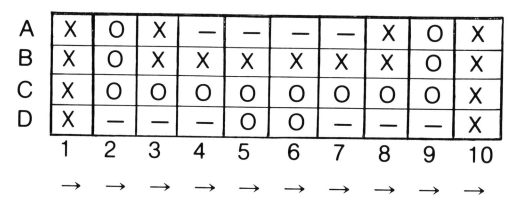

	1	2	3	4	5	6	7	8	9	10
A	X	O	X	—	—	—	—	X	O	X
B	X	O	X	X	X	X	X	X	O	X
C	X	O	O	O	O	O	O	O	O	X
D	X	—	—	—	O	O	—	—	—	X

→ → → → → → → → → →

Figure 41. *Pattern draft for Sample Band A. Three color values are indicated: x = dark, — = medium, o = light.*

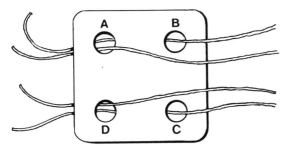

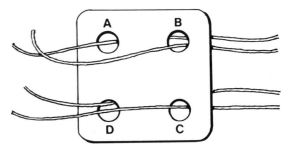

Figure 42. *When you thread the card from the front (lettered side) to the back, you are threading from left to right (the arrow points from left to right).*

Figure 43. *When you thread the card from the back (unlettered side) to the front, you are threading from right to left (the arrow points from right to left).*

(front to back), and an arrow to the left means that you thread the card from right to left (back to front). The pattern draft for Sample Band A calls for all cards to be threaded from left to right, or from front to back. If an individual card doesn't have all holes threaded from the same direction, the card won't turn. You'll find a more detailed discussion of threading in Chapter 4.

Colors

In card weaving, the threads that show, or those that make up the pattern, are the warp threads. The arrangement of colors in your warp threads, then, determines the design. Later, when you begin to draft your own patterns, you'll be able to choose colors either before or after drafting the pattern. Although you're asked, for clarity, to use the color values (dark, medium, and light) called for in weaving Sample Band A, color choice is always up to the individual, and there are no rules. Strongly contrasting colors are generally best for the beginning weaver, since strong contrast allows for easy visibility and simplicity in weaving. Very subtle color arrangements can be rich and brightly patterned, but are not as easy to work with.

The Warp Threads

The warp threads, those running through the cards, should be about half again as long as the desired length of the final woven piece. For instance, a 4-foot (48″) belt would require warp threads about 6 feet (72″) long. To weave Sample Band A, you'll need 40 warp threads, 16 dark, 14 light, and 10 medium, each 6 feet (72″) long.

Warping Instructions

It's important that all these strands be the same length and the best way to achieve this is to wrap a warp between two stationary objects. The next best thing to a weaver's warping board (Figure 44) is two C-clamps attached to a bench or table, adjusted to the right distance, and anchored securely (Figure 45).

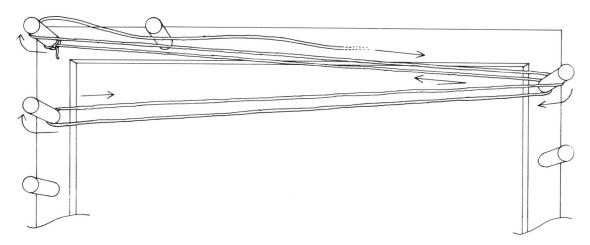

Figure 44. Wrapping warp threads on a weaver's warping board.

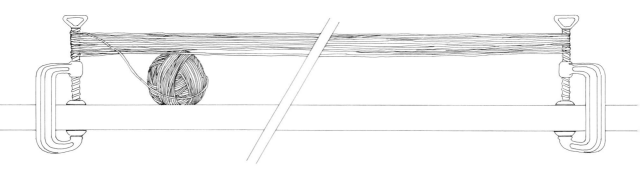

Figure 45. Wrapping warp threads between C-clamps.

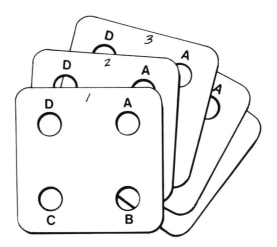

Figure 46. The weaving cards numbered in sequence between holes D and A.

Numbering the Cards

Take the number of cards to be used in the weaving (10 cards for Sample Band A). Then number the cards (in pencil so they can be reused) consecutively by placing a numeral at the top of each card between letters A and D (Figure 46). It's important that the cards, once numbered, be kept in order and stacked so that card 1 is on top.

Threading the Cards

As you begin to thread the cards you should have them stacked in front of you, with card 1 on the top. The warp threads should be laid out with one end of each thread near the stack of cards (Figure 47). The pattern draft tells you what color-value thread goes through each hole, and the arrows at the bottom of the pattern draft show you which direction the threads go through each card.

The draft for Sample Band A shows that card 1 requires 4 dark threads, card 2 takes light threads through holes A, B, and C, and a medium thread in hole D, and so on. In this pattern draft all the arrows point to the right, which means that you thread all the cards from front to back (left to right).

Begin by threading all the holes in card 1 with the appropriate color-value warp threads. Pull each warp thread through the hole for about 10". When card 1 is completely threaded place it face down beside the stack, then completely thread card 2. Place it face down on top of card 1, thread and stack card 3 in the same way, and so on with all the cards. It's important that the cards be stacked according to their consecutive numbers and that they be carefully kept in consistent order. Coloring the top edge (holes D and A) of each card will make it much easier to see when a card is out of order.

When all the cards have been threaded and are all face down before you, carefully hold them together with a strong rubber band. Take the warp threads where they have been threaded through the cards for 10", tie them securely into a knot, and anchor the knot to a secure hook or object (Figure 48). It's important for the lettered sides of the cards face toward the left.

Combing Out the Warp Threads

To start weaving, you'll have to pull the cards the length of the warp, and begin weaving at the end that isn't yet knotted and anchored. To do this, slip the rubber band from the cards and start moving the cards away from the anchor point, and toward the unknotted end of the warp. Hold and move them together as a loose bundle. As the warp threads slip through the holes in the cards, they'll be combed out and put in order. If you jiggle the cards and comb the warp threads with your fingers, the cards should move along and slide over the warp threads quite easily (Figure 49). If the threads become tangled, or if you must stop, place the rubber band around the cards to keep them in order and together. Use your fingers to comb out badly tangled pieces.

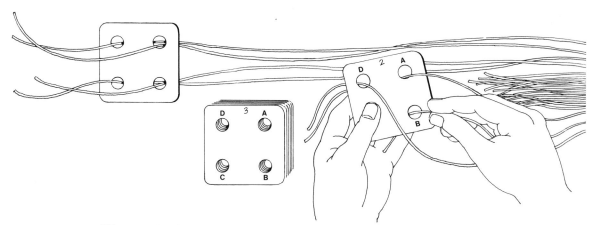

Figure 47. *The cards are threaded beginning with card 1, and then placed face down on the table.*

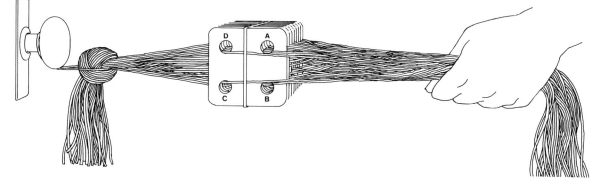

Figure 48. *Securing the knot to the anchor point. If the cards do not face to the weaver's left, then the expected pattern will be on the bottom of the weaving.*

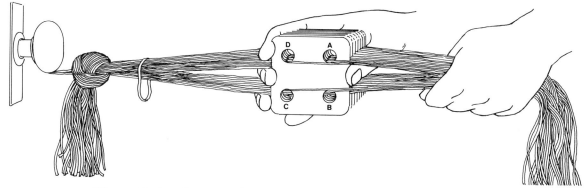

Figure 49. *Combing out the warp threads.*

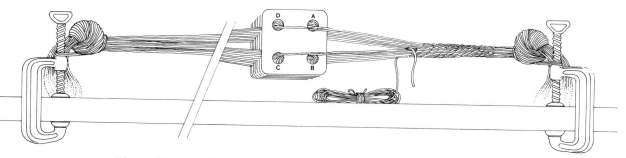

Figure 50. *A card weaving worked between two C-clamps.*

The warp should now be stretched out before you and the cards should be within 10″ of the unknotted end of the warp. The front or lettered sides of the cards must still face your left. Hold the unknotted warp ends firmly together, making sure that all the threads are in order and under equal tension. When the threads are in good order, knot the ends of the warp threads together as you did earlier with the other end.

The Weft Thread

The weft thread holds the warp threads together and doesn't show on the finished piece, except along the very edges. It's usually best for the weft thread to be the same color as the threads going through the first and last cards in the stack. Otherwise it will appear as irregular spots along the edge of the finished weaving. The weft thread can be the same material as used for the warp, or it can be a thinner material.

The weft thread should be wound onto a flat shuttle, or into a butterfly, so it can be passed easily through the shed while weaving. When you begin weaving, the weft thread may be pushed firmly into place with your fingers, a kitchen knife, or the edge of a shuttle (see Chapter 2).

Securing the Warp

With both ends of the warp knotted, the threads smooth and even, and one end anchored firmly, you're ready to secure the other end to your waist. You may use any comfortable means of securing the warp to your waist. Before you get "tied down" be sure that your pattern draft and weft thread are within easy reach. Some weavers prefer to remain free of the weaving by stretching the warp threads between two solid points (Figure 50).

Check to be certain that the cards all face left, that the cards are numerically consecutive from card 1, and that the DA holes in your cards are all on the top. Also, remove the rubber band from the cards or they won't turn properly.

Turning the Cards

When you have one end of the warp secured to the anchor point and the other end secured to your waist, test the possible tension by moving slightly backward and forward. With the tension reasonably tight, turn the cards as a unit one quarter turn toward your body (Figure 51). Test the shed thus created (Figure 52) between you and the cards by slipping your hand through, and return the cards to their original position. Then try a quarter-turn away from your body, again testing the shed (Figure 53). Move the cards back and forth to open the shed. Remember to keep the cards loosely packed and to turn them as a unit. As you turn the cards a slight jiggle will help them move freely. If an individual card doesn't turn, make certain that the card is threaded properly. Keep in mind that each "turn" is really only a quarter-turn of the cards.

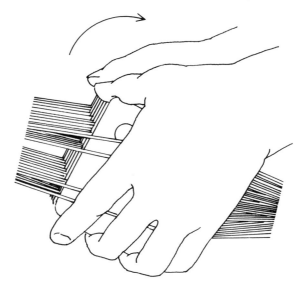

Figure 51. Turning the cards toward your body. The thumbs are placed on the top back, the fingers on the bottom.

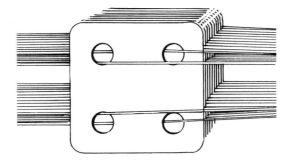

Figure 52. The weaving shed is the open space formed between the threads going through the top holes and the threads going through the bottom holes.

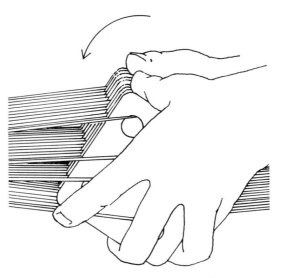

Figure 53. Turning the cards away from your body. The thumbs are on the top front, the fingers on the bottom.

Beginning to Weave

Begin by holding the cards in the neutral position, with holes DA on top. Slip the weft thread through the shed between the cards and your body, with the loose end hanging about 6″ out of the shed (Figure 54). Turn the cards one turn toward your body, return the weft thread back through the new shed, and turn the cards another turn toward your body, again slipping the weft thread through, and so on. You should turn the cards toward your body four turns in all, each time passing the weft thread through the newly created shed. Then turn the cards four turns away from your body, passing the weft thread through the shed each time, and so on. The shed opens best when the cards are pulled toward you, then pushed away. Figure 55 shows the first eight turns of the cards.

After you've woven for a short while you should be able at any time to know which way the next turn of the cards should go. As you weave Sample Band A, you'll find that as you turn the cards toward you, a design emerges and as you turn the cards away from you the mirror image appears. As you proceed, the designs form links (Figure 56).

When the cards turn, each set of four warp threads twist around themselves on both sides of the cards. As you weave, this twist produces an especially strong and attractive fabric. As you turn the cards toward you and away, the threads on the other side of the cards twist and untwist. If you don't turn the cards as many times in one direction as in the other, or if you miss turns, the twists will begin to distort the threads and cause difficulty. When this happens, you must either reverse the turning direction of the cards, or untie the anchored end of the warp and comb out the twists.

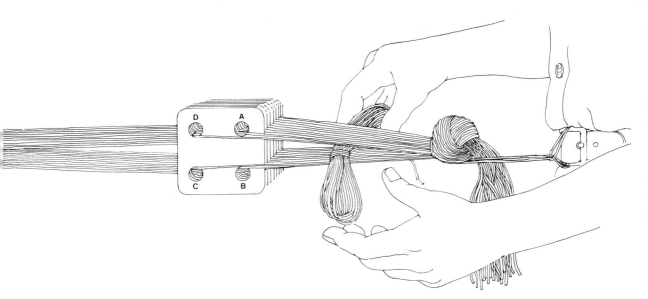

Figure 54. The cards, the warp threads, and the weaving shed in relation to the weaver.

Figure 55. *The first eight turns of the cards. After each turn, the weaver opens, or clears, the shed, passes the weft thread through the shed, and packs the weft thread firmly into place before making the next turn.*

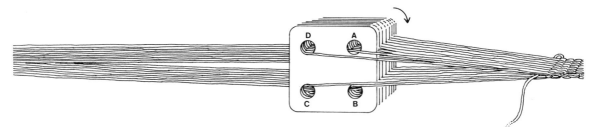

1. The neutral position. Holes D and A are at the top. It is in this position that the weft thread is first passed through the cleared shed.

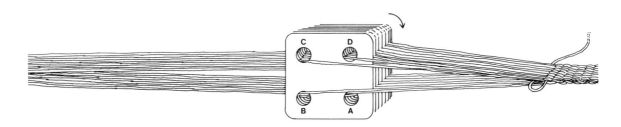

2. The first turn toward your body brings hole C to the top, so that holes C and D are now on the top.

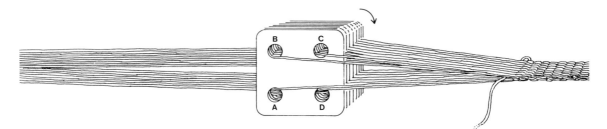

3. The second turn toward your body. Holes B and C are now on top.

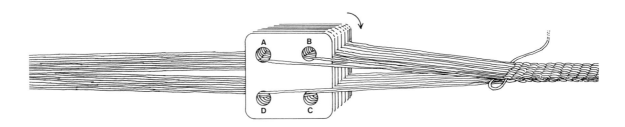

4. The third turn toward your body. Holes A and B are now on top.

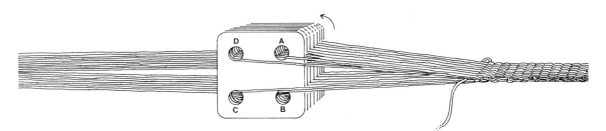

5. *The fourth turn toward your body, holes D and A are now on top.*

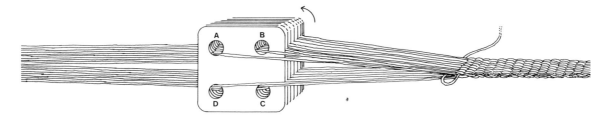

6. *The first turn away from your body, holes A and B are now on top.*

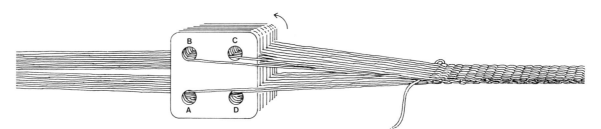

7. *The second turn away from your body, holes B and C are now on top.*

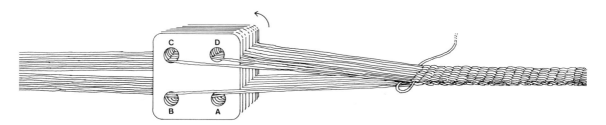

8. *The third turn away from your body, holes C and D are now on top.*

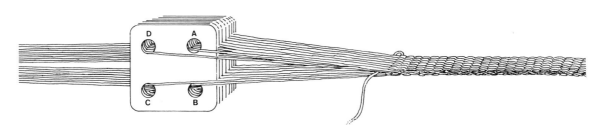

9. *The fourth turn away from your body brings the neutral position to the top.*

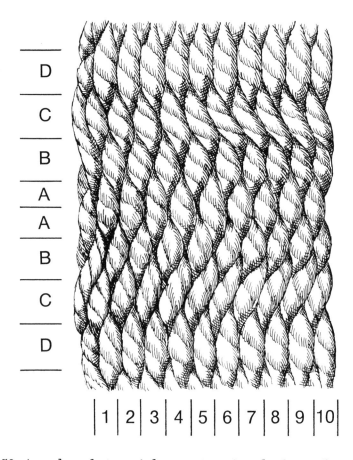

D C B A A B C D

| 1 | 2 | 3 | 4 | 5 | 6 | 7 | 8 | 9 | 10 |

Figure 56. An enlarged view of the weaving after the first eight turns. Rows one through four were created when the cards were turned toward the weaver's body, rows five through eight when the cards were turned away from the weaver's body.

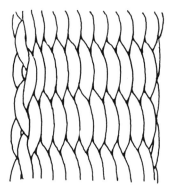

Figure 57. The weft thread "turning the corners" smoothly and snugly.

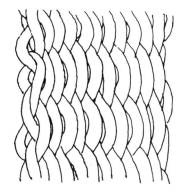

Figure 58. A rough, uneven edge resulting from sloppy weaving.

Controlling the Weft Thread

There's a feeling for this kind of weaving that comes with practice, and with sensitivity to the materials and to the importance of good craftsmanship. As you weave, pull the weft thread tightly enough so it goes smoothly into the next shed, but not so tight that it cramps the edges or causes the middle area to bunch up. The weft thread acts to bind the warp threads together and it keeps the weaving flat and the edges straight. It should pull the warp threads close enough together that they cover the weft. It's most important that the weft thread go "around the corners" snugly. The weft thread should be beaten firmly into place immediately after it's placed in its new shed. If not attended to properly, the weft thread will cause the weaving to become loose and the pattern indistinct (Figures 57 and 58).

Taking Up

As you work, the weaving will appear between your body and the cards. As the weaving continues you'll have to lean over to reach the new shed. When leaning becomes uncomfortable, untie the weaving (for it's now a weaving, not a bundle of warp threads) from your body, and retie it closer to the cards.

Finishing

Continue weaving until the sample is long enough, or until the cards are too close to the knot to turn. Untie the knot, slip the cards off, and secure the weft thread by tying it to one of the border warp threads, or by threading it back into the weaving. Card weaving is tight and dense enough that no special precautions need be taken to avoid unraveling. When you slip it from your waist you'll be holding the completed weaving.

Problems and Mistakes in Weaving

Clearing the Shed. For a good shed, the warp threads must be under strong and even tension. Move the cards once toward you and once away in a smooth, easy movement. This movement helps to open the shed, but must be done smoothly and evenly. Frantic or harsh movement will tend to shred the warp. The cards should be worked as a unit, and must be "square," not uneven (Figure 59).

Turning the Cards. As you attempt to turn the cards beware of loose tension, of cards too tightly packed together, and of individual cards incorrectly threaded. Cards turn most easily on smooth threads, less easily on threads that are thick or fuzzy.

Repairing Broken Warp Threads. Use a secure knot to attach a new warp strand to the broken thread. Tie the knot as close to the woven area as possible. Thread the new warp strand properly through the card and carry it along to the anchor point, adjust the tension, and tie (be careful).

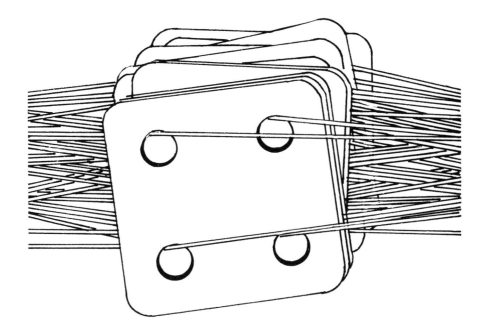

Figure 59. An unclear shed.

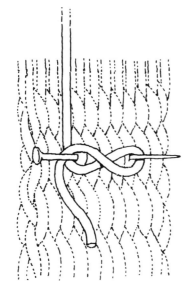

Figure 60. Replacing a warp thread broken and lost in the weaving.

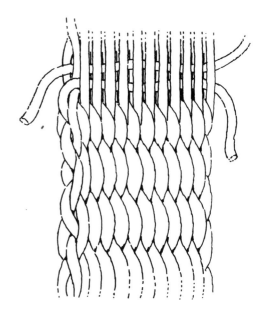

Figure 61. A new weft thread over-laping the old one.

If the warp thread breaks within the weaving, pin a new warp thread in place and continue weaving (Figure 60). When the weaving is completed, unpin the new warp thread and use a needle or crochet hook to weave the end back into the piece. You can avoid broken warp strands by choosing strong threads, and by being gentle with them once you begin to weave. Yarn sometimes comes from the factory with knots—be sure to avoid using these lengths in your warp strands. Thin threads may be doubled for extra strength. Some weavers find commercially manufactured fabric glue helpful in repairing broken threads.

Starting a new weft thread in the traditional method, old and new weft threads are passed through the same shed and packed firmly together (Figure 61). The ends of both threads, when possible, should be allowed to extend about 6″ beyond the weaving. Wool threads generally bind well and the weft ends may be cut flush with the edge after several more rows of weaving. Cotton and other smooth materials slip more easily, and might have to be pulled back through the weaving, so should not be cut until obviously secure.

Mistakes in Weaving. Most card weaving errors occur as a result of incorrect turning of the cards, and of inaccurate threading of the cards when setting up the weaving. Always be doubly certain that the correct color is threaded through the right hole in each card. As you gain experience, understanding, and "feel" you'll work more and more accurately and confidently.

When a mistake does occur you probably won't notice it until you've woven several rows beyond it. If you make a mistake on your first weaving it would probably be best to understand the cause of your error, and then continue weaving.

Taking out a woven section to get at an error can be very frustrating, and can cause even greater problems. When you must take out a section of weaving you'll, essentially, be weaving backward (or unweaving). To do this, move the border card on the side from which the weft protrudes in such a way as to open the shed and free the weft thread. Use this border card as a guide, and follow by moving all the remaining cards into the position of the guide border card. Threads often become very firmly entwined during weaving, so removing the weft thread can sometimes, especially with wool, require considerable force.

Figure 62. (Right) Woolen wall hanging, 7" x 60", by Donna Armstrong.

Figure 63. (Below) Woolen belt, 1½" wide, by Robert Cranford.

Figure 64. *Woolen wall hanging, 5″ x 33″, by Liz Brierly.*

4. PATTERN DRAFTING AND DESIGNING

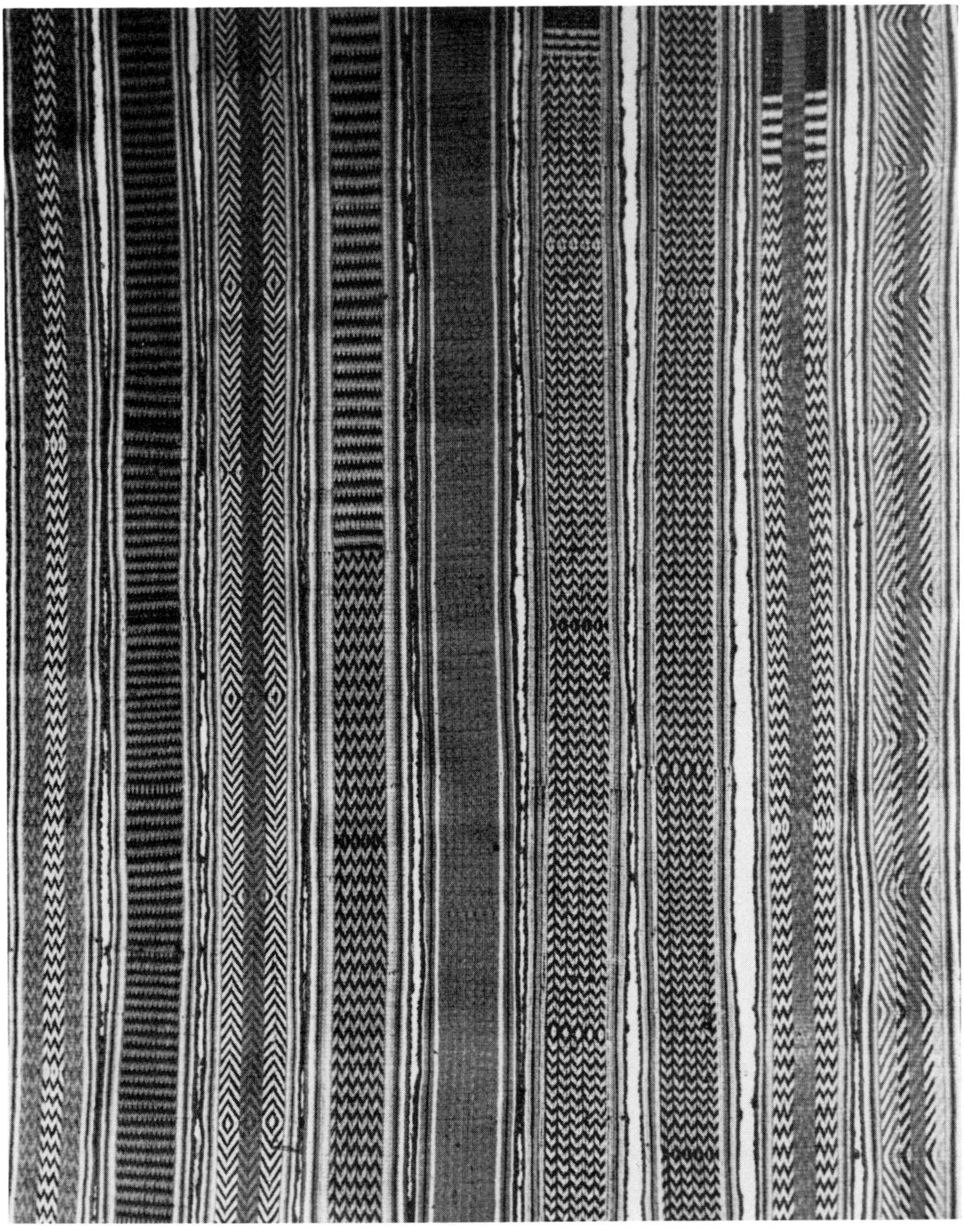

Figure 65. *Contemporary Tibetan cotton bands, each 2″ wide. Each card—except for the border cards—was threaded with two dark threads and two light threads.*

There are two basic approaches to pattern design for card weaving. The first method requires working the pattern out carefully on graph paper, using as many different colors and shapes as desired, and threading each card according to the graph. In the second method, described by means of a sampler that includes a special way of warping, each card is threaded with dark threads through holes A and B and light threads through holes C and D. The design is worked and changed by varying the turning sequences, by turning individual cards, and by "flipping" cards to change the threading direction.

Defining the Design Space

The grid in Figure 66 shows the design space for a weaving that would require 11 four-holed cards. The letters A, B, C, and D each represent one hole on each card; the numbers across the bottom each represent an individual card. Each square in the grid represents the point at which a warp thread will show on the surface of the completed weaving. There are 44 squares in the grid, just as there are a total of 44 holes in the 11 cards being used and 44 warp threads in the weaving.

Designing the Pattern

The squares of the sample grid shown in Figure 66 may be filled in with symbols that represent a complex pattern of many colors, or simpler designs may be developed with just two or three colors. However complex or simple, designs are worked up easily on such a grid. If all the holes in both of the "border" cards (cards 1 and 11 in Figure 66) are threaded with strands the same color as the weft thread, the weft thread won't stand out, or "show." The weaving from this pattern can involve the simple four forward, four back turning of the cards, or it can incorporate a repetition or series of repetitions of any design element. The simple triangular, two-color design shown in Figure 67 is again shown in Figure 68 as it would appear if the cards were turned four turns toward the weaver, four turns away, and then eight turns toward the weaver. The woven design can be changed greatly by alternating or supplementing the regular four-turn series with one, two, three, five, or more turns before reversing. The series of turns may also be erratic, with three forward, five back, etc. In Figure 68, #3 and #4 show how the pattern will look when the cards are turned eight turns toward the body.

The pattern draft shows which color thread goes through each card hole. Different colors can be indicated by symbols or by coloring in squares with colored pencils or felt tip markers.

Threading the Cards

The direction of the twist of each warp thread is an important element of the design and texture of the finished weaving. It's determined by the

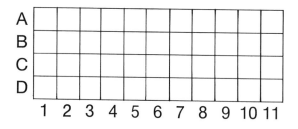

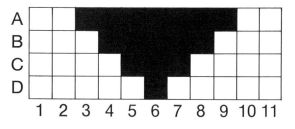

Figure 66. *The design space defined for a pattern draft. The letters A,B,C, and D down the left-hand side represent the lettered holes on a square card. Each of the numbers 1 through 11 across the bottom represents an individual card. Each horizontal row represents one row of weaving.*

Figure 67. *A two-color design is formed by filling in part of the design area.*

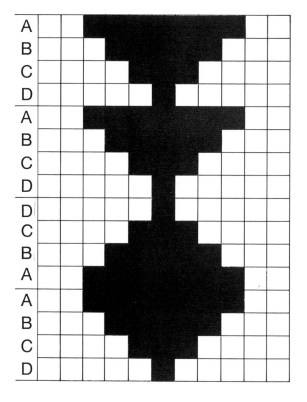

Figure 68. *A graphed illustration of how the design in Figure 67 will appear when woven. Section 1, the first four rows, represents the image that will appear when the cards are turned toward the weaver's body: row D appears first, then C, then B, then A. Section 2, woven with the cards rotating away from the body, will be a mirror image. Sections 3 and 4 represent a graphed version of how the design would progress if the weaver chose to turn the cards eight (rather than the usual four) turns toward the body.*

Figure 69. These graphs show five possible ways of arranging and threading one basic pattern. Figure 70 shows how each of these patterns look when woven. Figure 71 shows the back or underneath side of these same weavings.

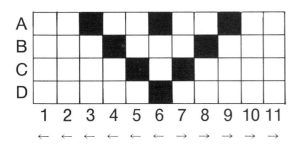

1. *This threading produces a smooth-angled design.*

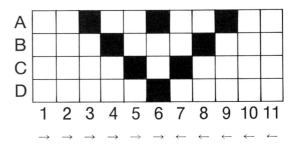

2. *This threading produces a broken-angled design.*

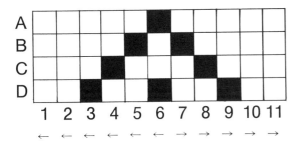

3. *This threading produces a broken-angled design.*

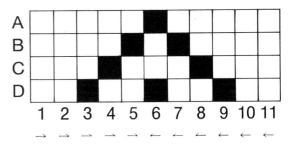

4. *This threading produces a smooth-angled design.*

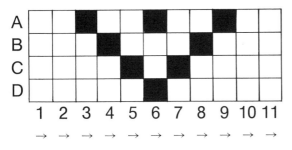

5. *This threading produces a smooth-angled design on the right side of the weaving and a broken angle on the left.*

direction from which the warp threads enter the cards, and each pattern draft shows these threading instructions.

All four holes on each card must be threaded from the same direction, but each card may be threaded from either left or right, regardless of how the other cards are threaded. The small arrows under the numbers along the bottom of the pattern draft (see Figure 69) tell whether the warp strands will enter the card from left to right or right to left. When threading, hold the card so that the lettered, or left, side faces to your left. If the arrow points left to right the card will be threaded from the lettered side to the blank side. If the arrow goes to the left, take the four strands through from right to left (or from the blank side to the lettered side). A mixed threading direction on one card will prevent the card from turning. If a pattern has only horizontal and vertical lines the cards can be threaded either all one way or all the other way. If a pattern has oblique angles, as in Figure 67, the woven design can change radically depending on how it's threaded. Figure 69 shows five different ways of arranging and threading a similar design. Figure 70 shows how these threadings appear when woven on the top surface, and Figure 71 shows the appearance of the back or underneath surface.

The threading direction also determines whether a line that angles obliquely in the pattern will be smooth or broken. Figure 72 shows how each thread will angle during weaving if threaded according to the arrows (see Figure 69, #1). Notice that the threads angle one way when the cards are turned toward the body (Figure 72, #1) and just the opposite when turned away (Figure 72, #2). Oblique angles can be threaded to give a smooth line or a broken line, and these elements can be very important in the design. If the angles are threaded to be smooth on the surface, they'll be broken on the underneath or bottom side. Compare the weavings in Figure 70 with their bottom surfaces shown in Figure 71. Changes of threading from one card to the next can create subtle design variations and should be experimented with. Paired, or alternate, threading means that the threading direction is changed with each card. This method of threading gives a woven surface with the appearance of knitting (Figure 76). At the point during weaving where the threading direction is changed (between cards 6 and 7 on the graphs in Figure 69) the weft thread, which usually remains hidden in the weaving, will show on the woven surface as a short horizontal bar every eight rows if the cards are turned four turns toward the body and four turns away from the body (see Figure 77). If the cards are turned continuously in one direction the weft won't appear. This small horizontal bar can be an important design element, and sometimes the color and weight of the weft should be chosen on this basis.

The completion of the pattern draft is only the beginning, since many design elements can be introduced as the weaving develops. Once the cards are threaded and work begins, the weaver can change and elaborate on the design by turning the cards in different sequences, by turning individual cards (Figure 78) and in the many other ways shown throughout this book.

Figure 70. These rayon bands, each 1" wide, are samples of the graphed patterns in Figure 69. Pattern 1 is on the left and Pattern 5 is on the right.

Figure 71. The back of the sample bands shown in Figure 70.

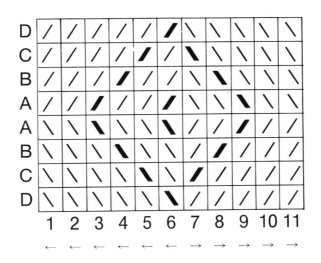

Figure 72. The individual threads in card weaving twist to the right or left depending on the direction from which the cards were threaded. This pattern shows how the threads will angle as the cards are turned four turns toward the body and four turns away. Cards 1 through 6 are threaded to the left and will angle to the left when the cards are turned toward the body, and toward the right when the cards are turned away. Cards 7 through 11 are threaded to the right and will do just the opposite. This graph shows how the threads in Figure 69, #1 will angle.

Figure 73. *A wool band, 1½" wide, in a pattern that combines angles and horizontal lines. The pattern has been threaded to make the individual threads angle in the same direction as the edges of the diamond-shaped design. The edges of the design are smooth, as compared to the broken design angle on the reverse surface.*

Figure 74. *The back of Figure 73. The angled diamond pattern is distinct but not smooth. Notice that the twist of threads is counter to the angle of design.*

Figure 75. *Detail of two wool bands, each 1½" wide, by Joyce Wexler. All the warp threads for both bands were threaded from left to right. Compare the threading pattern of the left-hand band with that shown in Figure 73.*

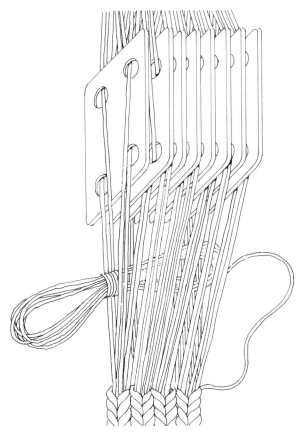

Figure 76. *When cards are threaded in pairs as in Figure 83, the weaving produced has the appearance of knitting.*

Figure 77. *Detail of both sides of a wool band, 1½″ wide. The weft thread shows as short, black horizontal lines on the weaving surface at the points where the threading direction of the cards changed.*

Figure 78. *A wool belt based on the diamond motif, 1½″ wide, by Ricardo Mata. Individual cards were turned to put colored warp threads in different positions.*

Selecting Colors

There are no strict rules for using colors, but a few suggestions might be helpful. Strongly contrasting colors allow the pattern to show clearly and are easiest for beginners to work with. Colors with less striking contrast create more subtle, warmer designs. Many weavers prefer a light, dark, and medium value in their colors. A strong dark area can be divided into dark colors which, while maintaining the dark shape, add variety and interest.

Begin with colors you like and if the colors arranged in a pattern turn out to be unsatisfactory, play with the design by turning the cards in vari-

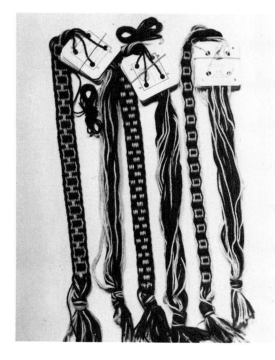

Figure 79. The pattern for Sample Band A (Chapter 3) was used for each of these bands, with the same colors in different positions.

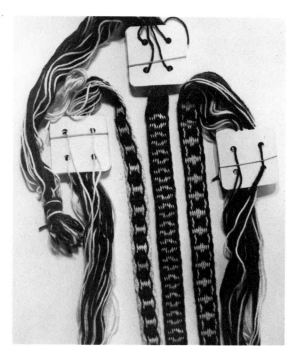

Figure 80. The back of the bands shown in Figure 79.

	1	2	3	4	5	6	7	8	9	10	11
A	−	O	X	/	S	S	S	/	X	O	−
B	S	−	O	X	/	S	/	X	O	−	S
C	/	S	−	O	X	/	X	O	−	S	/
D	/	/	S	−	O	X	O	−	S	/	/

← ← ← ← ← ← → → → → →

Figure 81. Considerably less complicated than it at first appears, this is basically the same pattern as given in Figure 67, but with five symbols, each of which stands for a separate color. The X's represent the outline of the basic pattern.

ous ways. Always watch the bottom surface of the weaving, since unexpectedly attractive patterns often appear there that are quite different from the top pattern. The placement of a particular color can change the appearance of a design. Figures 79 and 80 show how the different placements of white affect the design in one pattern. Figure 81 shows the simple two-color pattern found in Figure 67 complicated by the addition of color. The outline shape is evident in the x's, and this outline is followed with different colored lines paralleling the primary design element. The resulting pattern, if the cards are turned normally (four forward and four back), will be a pattern of diamonds within diamonds similar to Figure 82.

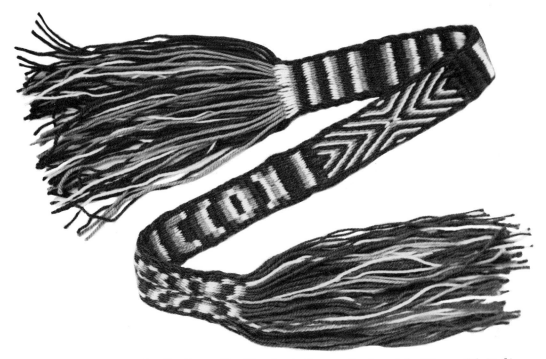

Figure 82. A sampler by Janet Becklund, similar to the band in Figure 85. Half the cards were threaded to the right and half to the left. Two dark colors and two light colors were used.

A	X	X	X	X	X	X	X	X	X	X	X	X	X	X	X	X	X	X	X	X
B	X	X	X	X	X	X	X	X	X	X	X	X	X	X	X	X	X	X	X	X
C	O	O	O	O	O	O	O	O	O	O	O	O	O	O	O	O	O	O	O	O
D	O	O	O	O	O	O	O	O	O	O	O	O	O	O	O	O	O	O	O	O
	1	2	3	4	5	6	7	8	9	10	11	12	13	14	15	16	17	18	19	20

→ ← → ← → ← → ← → ← → ← → ← → ← → ← → ←

Figure 83. A graph of the pattern produced by threading the cards as illustrated in Figure 84. The cards end up threaded in pairs. All even-numbered cards are threaded to the left, all odd-numbered cards to the right. All A and B holes have dark threads, all C and D holes light threads.

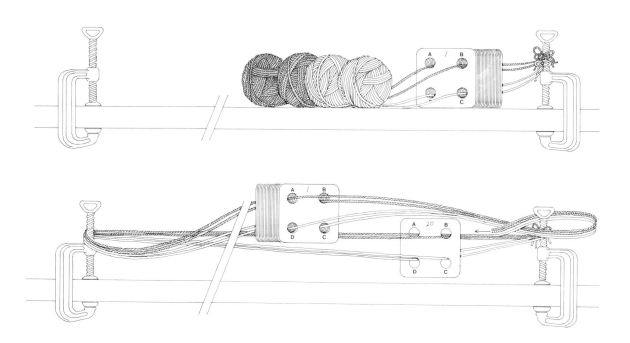

Figure 84. (Above) Wrapping a warp by dropping cards. The warp is wrapped, combed, and the cards are threaded all at the same time. Four balls of yarn are used, with each yarn end going through one hole of each card. The cards are stacked in numerical order with card Number 1 on the top. As the warp is drawn through the cards and brought around a C-clamp, a card is dropped into position beginning with the last card, in this case Number 20. In this illustration dark threads go through holes A and B, and light threads through C and D.

Figure 85. (Right) Sample Band B made with 3-ply wool rug yarn by the author. The band was woven in two sections beginning on the bottom left and ending on the top right.

Sample Band B: Experimenting with Design

Card weaving is a flexible technique where designs may be created and formed as the weaving progresses. Many card weavers find that the simple threading technique described in Sample Band B, using two dark threads and two light, offers such a wide range of possibilities that they use it almost exclusively. The instructions that follow are just an introduction to its nearly unlimited range of possibilities.

Preparing the Warp

The pattern draft for Sample Band B is shown in Figure 83. This sampler can be set up and threaded according to instructions in Chapter 3 or by a much speedier method of warping where the wrapping of the warp, the combing of the warp, and the threading of the cards are done simultaneously. When this method of warping (Figure 84) is used the cards will be threaded from alternate directions, and all the A holes will have the same color, all the B holes the same color, and so on. Take 20 cards numbered consecutively and stack the cards with number 1 on top. Select two colors (dark and light) and wind each color into two balls. Take the stack of cards and thread one dark thread through all the A holes, one dark thread through the B holes, one light thread through the C holes, and one light thread through the D holes, as shown in Figure 92. Using two C-clamps placed about 80″ apart, begin by tying the 4 yarn ends to the right-hand C-clamp. (The sampler can be done in two sections, each 50″ in length, as the sampler in Figure 85 was done. The sampler was done with 3-ply wool rug yarn. A lighter-weight yarn would require less length.)

Put the four balls of yarn in a box or basket to keep them from rolling. Hold the stack of cards facing you and slide the last card (card 20) from the bottom of the stack near the right-hand C-clamp, as illustrated. Bring the remaining cards, which will simultaneously comb out the warp, around the left C-clamp and back, dropping off another card (card 19) from the bottom of the stack as the warp threads and cards are brought past card 20. Each time the warp threads pass by the dropped cards, another card is dropped from the bottom, until all the cards have been dropped into the newly formed stack. Tie the thread ends to the right-hand C-clamp. The cards and warp are now prepared for weaving.

Weaving Sample Band B

Step 1. To weave a band similar to Sample Band B, begin by turning the cards four turns toward your body and four turns away. This produces the simple horizontal stripes visible in the bottom left of Figure 85.

Step 2. With holes A and B on top, turn a weaving sequence of quarter turns as follows: AB toward the body, AB on top, AB away from the body. Continue weaving in this manner for 2″. The top surface of the weaving will be dark and the bottom light (this is double-face weaving, and is discussed in more detail in Chapter 6).

Step 3. With holes A and B on top, individually turn cards 5, 6, 7, 8, and 13, 14, 15, 16 two quarter-turns toward the body. This puts holes C and D on top. Weave as in step 2 for 2″. This produces vertical stripes.

Step 4. Keeping the cards in their new position, weave four turns toward the body and four turns away for 2″. This produces checks.

Step 5. Turn cards 5 through 8, and 13 through 16 back to their original positions by turning two quarter-turns away from the body. Weave as in step 2 for 1″.

Step 6. With holes A and B on top, turn the two center cards, card 10 and card 11, upside down by turning two quarter-turns toward the body. Weave one sequence as in step 2 (AB on top, AB toward the body, AB on top, AB away from the body). Take the two adjoining cards on each side of the two middle cards (8, 9, and 12, 13) and turn them upside down in the same manner as 10 and 11, and again weave the same sequence. Continue enlarging the "v" design by turning adjoining pairs and weaving until all but the border cards have been turned. Now reverse the process to form a diamond.

Step 7. Turn the cards sixteen turns away from the body without weaving. Move the cards toward the body after each quarter-turn to pack the resulting twists, but don't bring the weft thread across. Carry the weft thread up by wrapping it around the border spiral every fourth turn. Resume weaving and turn the cards sixteen turns away from the body. This will untwist the warp threads.

Step 8. To form diamonds within diamonds, arrange as follows:

Card 1 AB toward	Card 11 AB away
Card 2 AB top	Card 12 AB bottom
Card 3 AB away	Card 13 AB toward
Card 4 AB bottom	Card 14 AB top
Card 5 AB toward	Card 15 AB away
Card 6 AB top	Card 16 AB bottom
Card 7 AB away	Card 17 AB toward
Card 8 AB bottom	Card 18 AB top
Card 9 AB toward	Card 19 AB away
Card 10 AB top	Card 20 AB bottom

Weave a sequence of eight turns toward the body and eight turns away, then repeat. Now turn four turns toward and four turns away, then repeat.

Step 9. In order to form oblique jagged designs that angle to the left when the cards are turned toward the body, and to the right when the cards are turned away, flip all even-numbered cards as illustrated in Figure 86. When

Cape (Left) by the author. This cape was woven with wool yarn in strips with wrapped and overlapped sections. Patterns for some of the strips can be found in Chapter 5.

Detail of cape (Below).

Hanging (Top Left) by Phoebe McAfee. Woven in wool yarn, 15″ x 20″.

Hanging (Left) by Helene Durbin. Woven in horsehair, wool, and feathers, 9″ x 30″.

Neckpiece (Right) by the author. Woven in wool with inlaid karakul fleece.

Detail of purse by Roxanne Clarke. Woven in wool yarn, with wrapped fringe, 11" x 14". The pattern was adapted from an ancient Egyptian design.

Detail of serape by the author. Woven in strips with wool yarn.

Detail of scarf by Susan Boblitt. Woven in 3-ply wool rug yarn with six-holed cards, 6" wide. The pattern is shown in Chapter 5.

Detail of two bands by Janet Bucknam. Woven in wool yarn, each 2" wide. These bands use the same pattern but have different color arrangements.

Serape *by Robert Cranford. Combines card-woven strips with loom-woven fabric.*

Hanging by the author. Woven in horsehair, mohair, wool, and feathers, 18" x 30".

Detail of weaving by Lillian Elliott. Combines assorted materials with embroidery overlay.

Woven band by Helene Durbin. Woven with wool yarn, 4¾" wide. The band shows how changes of tension during weaving can create an angle in the fabric. The technique is discussed in Chapter 7.

Bands *by Ana Lisa Hedstrom. Woven with wool yarn, 3″ x 62″ and 2″ x 50″. These bands were woven in the double-face technique, explained in Chapter 6.*

Hanging *by Phoebe McAfee. Woven in one piece with wool yarn, 7″ x 48″.*

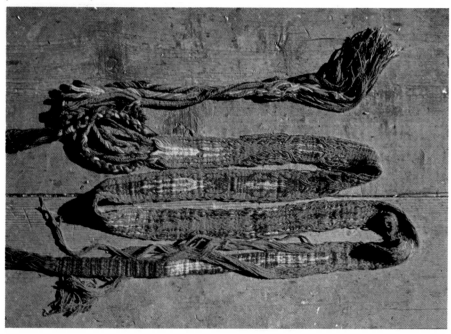

Belt *by Helene Durbin. Woven in cotton and linen yarns, 2″ wide. Some of the warp threads were tie-dyed before weaving.*

Hanging *by Lillian Elliott. Woven in mohair, alpaca, and camel hair strips, 72" x 120".*

flipped over, the cards will all be threaded from left to right. Weave by turning four turns toward, four away, four toward, eight away, and four toward the body. The angles on the bottom of the weaving will be smooth.

Step 10. Smooth, undulating waves or angles will appear on the weaving surface when the cards are positioned as graphed in Figure 87. To achieve this, position the two dark threads as follows:

Card 1 bottom	Card 11 top
Card 2 toward	Card 12 away
Card 3 top	Card 13 bottom
Card 4 away	Card 14 toward
Card 5 bottom	Card 15 top
Card 6 toward	Card 16 away
Card 7 top	Card 17 bottom
Card 8 away	Card 18 toward
Card 9 bottom	Card 19 top
Card 10 toward	Card 20 away

Turn the cards eight turns toward the body, so the threads and design will angle to the right, and eight turns away from the body, so the threads and design will angle to the left. Now, to finish the sample, turn four turns toward, and four turns away.

The card weavings in Figures 88, 89, and 90 have a threading similar to this. The large diagonals are created when an increasing number of cards are turned in one direction, and a decreasing number of cards are turned in the other direction. After every two turns a card is shifted from one group to the other.

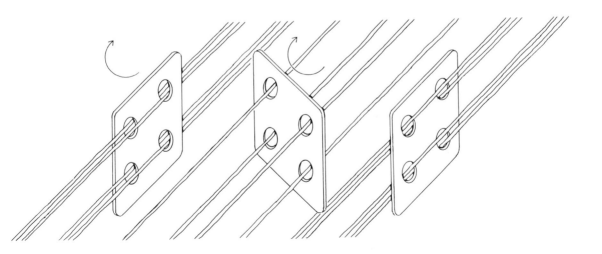

Figure 86. Cards can be flipped to change the threading direction. When a card is flipped the four warp threads are put into a new order.

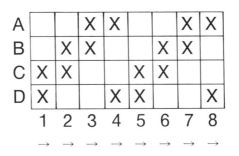

	1	2	3	4	5	6	7	8
A			X	X			X	X
B		X	X			X	X	
C	X	X			X	X		
D	X			X	X			X

→ → → → → → → →

Figure 87. A pattern with an angled design that goes to the right. Each card has two dark threads and two light threads. The direction of threading from left to right will produce a smooth angle on the weaving surface. If cards are threaded with two darks and two lights, individual cards can be turned to put the colors in the right place to produce this pattern. The threading direction can be changed as illustrated in Figure 86.

Figure 88. Four wool bands, each about 1½″ wide, by Gail Manners. Each card had two light threads and two dark threads. Variations in the bands were created by a complex system of turning the cards (an increasing number of cards are turned in one direction, while a decreasing number are turned in the other).

Figure 89. Detail of plied-cotton bands, 1" wide, woven by Flora Milligan and similar to those in Figure 90.

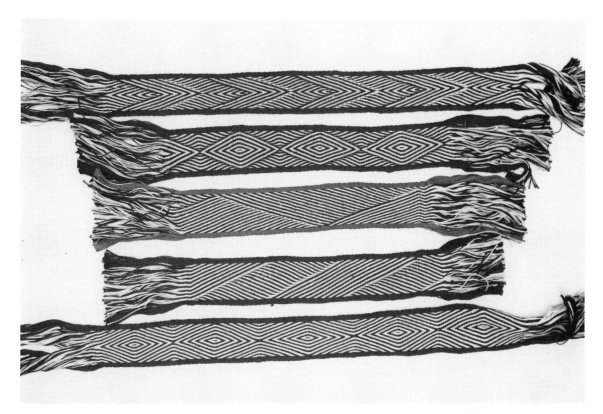

Figure 90. Fine, plied-cotton bands, each 1" wide, by Flora Milligan. The large diagonals were created by turning some cards toward the weaver and others away from the weaver.

Figure 91. A wool band, 2" wide, based on the diamond motif.

Figure 92. A sampler by Vera Brown, similar to the one in Figure 85 except that the cards were all threaded in one direction and the border cards were threaded in one color.

Figure 93. A wool band, 3½" wide, by Nancy Woodward.

Figure 94. A wool band, 1½″ wide, by the author.

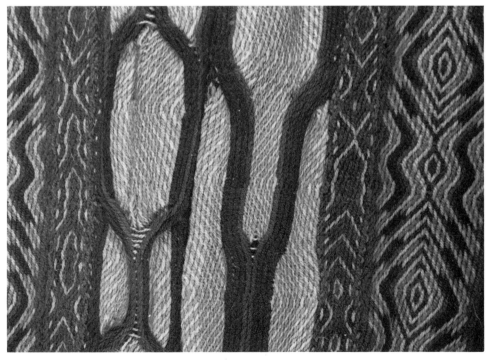

Figure 95. Two wool bands, each 3½″ wide, woven by the author. These are based on an angle pattern similar to the draft shown in Figure 87. A number of border cards were threaded in one color. Periodically these cards were picked up, moved laterally, and arranged in different positions, creating the strong linear movement superimposed over the subtly undulating pattern beneath.

5.   PATTERN DRAFTS

In this chapter you'll see a number of pattern drafts, along with descriptions and photographs of bands that were woven from them. These drafts were chosen for their variety as well as for their fullness and density. Many factors effect the final appearance of card-woven bands—even bands woven by different weavers from identical pattern drafts are seldom more than merely similar.

Just below each pattern draft is a description of the colors that the symbols in the draft represent, and a listing of the number of warp threads needed for each color. It's important that the weaver not feel restricted to the materials or colors listed, or to the position of a particular color within a weaving. Use the drafts as inspiration for the great variety of patterns possible in card weaving.

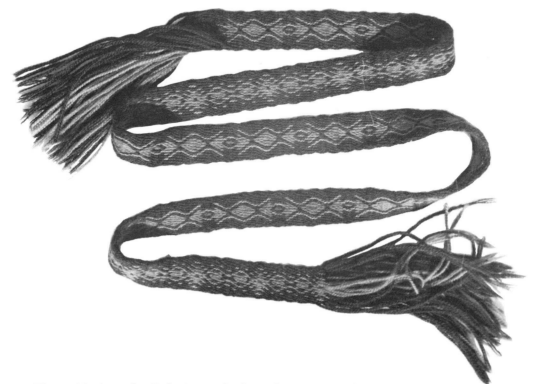

Figure 96. A woolen belt, 1½″ wide, by Robert Cranford.

Figure 97. Pattern Draft 1.

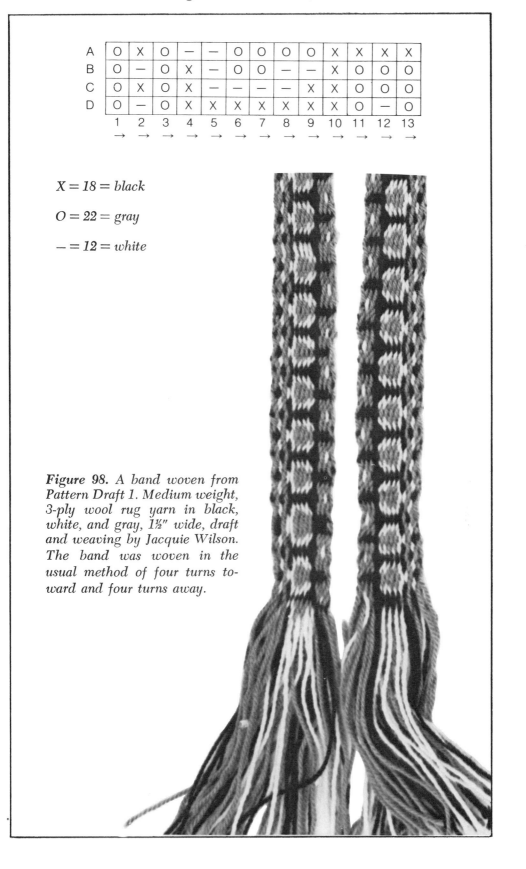

		1	2	3	4	5	6	7	8	9	10	11	12	13
A		O	X	O	—	—	O	O	O	O	X	X	X	X
B		O	—	O	X	—	O	O	—	—	X	O	O	O
C		O	X	O	X	—	—	—	—	X	X	O	O	O
D		O	—	O	X	X	X	X	X	X	X	O	—	O

$X = 18 = black$

$O = 22 = gray$

$— = 12 = white$

Figure 98. *A band woven from Pattern Draft 1. Medium weight, 3-ply wool rug yarn in black, white, and gray, 1½″ wide, draft and weaving by Jacquie Wilson. The band was woven in the usual method of four turns toward and four turns away.*

Figure 99. Pattern Draft 2.

	1	2	3	4	5	6	7	8	9	10	11	12	13	14	15	16	17	18	19	20	21	22	23	24
A	O	X	–	–	O	–	–	X	X	–	–	O	O	–	–	X	X	–	–	O	–	–	X	O
B	O	–	X	–	–	–	X	–	–	X	–	–	–	–	X	–	–	X	–	–	–	X	–	O
C	O	–	–	X	–	X	–	–	–	–	–	X	–	–	–	–	–	X	–	X	–	–	O
D	O	–	–	–	X	–	–	–	–	–	–	X	X	–	–	–	–	–	–	–	X	–	–	O

← ← ← ← ← → → → ← ← ← ← → → → → ← ← → → → → → →

X = 22 = black

O = 12 = red

– = 62 = white

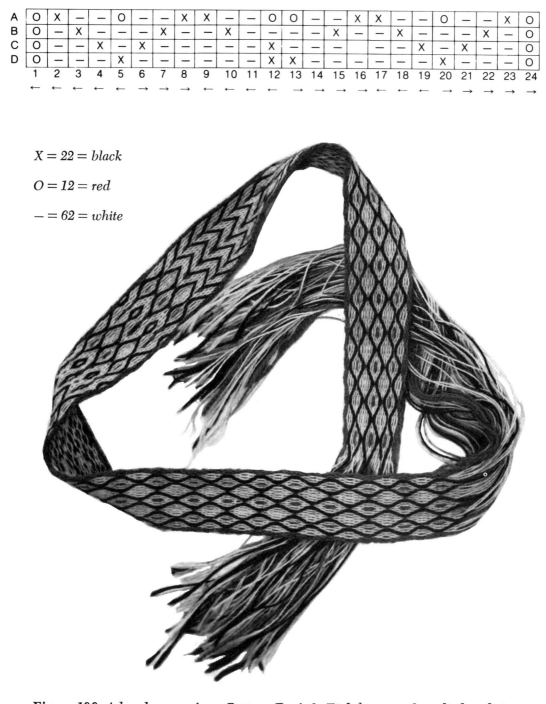

Figure 100. *A band woven from Pattern Draft 2. Tightly spun, fine-plied mohair in black and white, and fine 2-ply rug wool in red, 2″ wide, draft and weaving by the author. The beginning and end of the band were woven in the usual four turns toward the body and four away. The middle section shows the results of turning the cards arbitrarily out of the usual sequence. The red weft thread is an important part of the design.*

Figure 101. Pattern Draft 3.

	1	2	3	4	5	6	7	8	9	10	11	12	13	14	15	16	17	18	19	20
A	X	—	X	Z	S	O	X	P	P	P	X	W	W	X	O	S	Z	X	—	X
B	X	—	X	Z	S	O	X	P	P	P	X	W	W	X	O	S	Z	X	—	X
C	X	—	X	Z	S	O	X	X	X	X	P	X	X	X	O	S	Z	X	—	X
D	X	—	X	Z	S	O	O	O	O	X	P	O	O	O	O	S	Z	X	—	X
	→	→	→	→	→	→	→	→	→	→	→	→	→	→	→	→	→	→	→	→

$X = 30 = $ burgundy (dark red)

$— = 8 = $ blue

$Z = 8 = $ red (bright red)

$S = 8 = $ brown (light)

$O = 14 = $ orange

$P = 8 = $ green

$W = 4 = $ pink

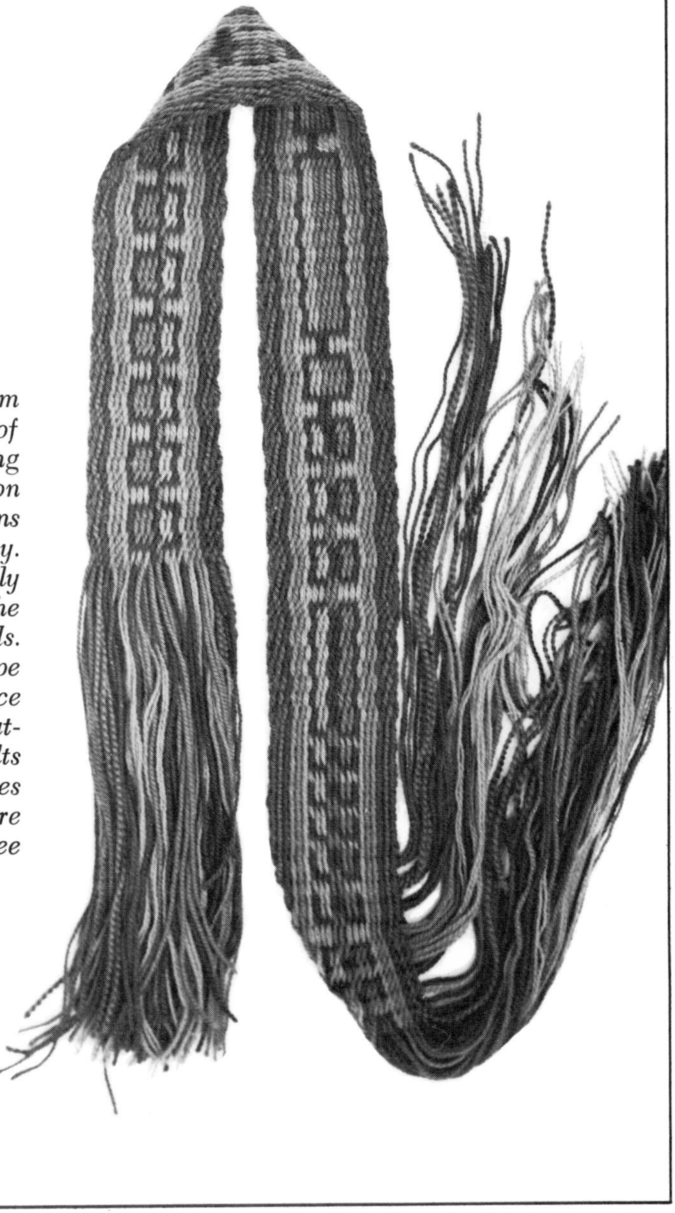

Figure 102. *A band woven from Pattern Draft 3. Various colors of plied wool yarn, draft and weaving by the author. The left section shows the pattern woven four turns toward the body and four away. Cards 17 and 18 are occasionally turned independently to change the position of the dark "X" threads. Near the top right, the box shape has been extended by double-face weaving (see Chapter 6). The pattern near the lower right results from turning the cards many times in one direction. Warp threads were decreased to narrow the band (see Chapter 7).*

Figure 103. Pattern Draft 4.

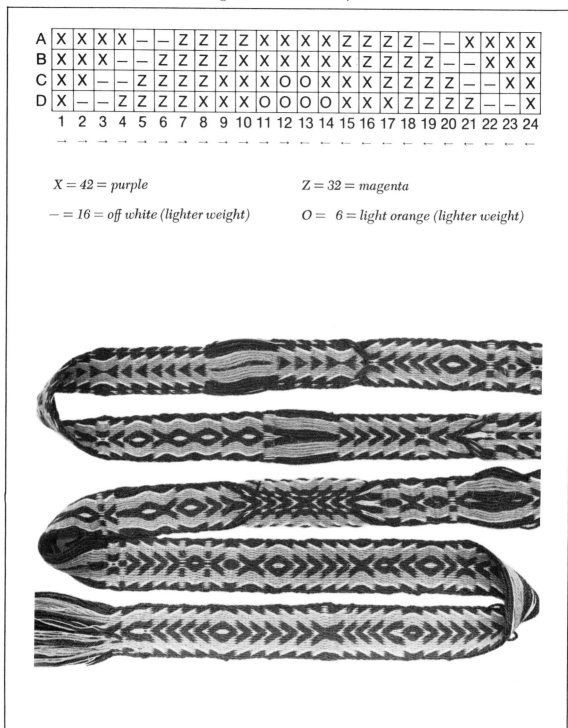

	1	2	3	4	5	6	7	8	9	10	11	12	13	14	15	16	17	18	19	20	21	22	23	24
A	X	X	X	X	—	—	Z	Z	Z	Z	X	X	X	X	Z	Z	Z	Z	—	—	X	X	X	X
B	X	X	X	—	—	Z	Z	Z	Z	X	X	X	X	X	X	Z	Z	Z	Z	—	—	X	X	X
C	X	X	—	—	Z	Z	Z	Z	X	X	X	O	O	X	X	X	Z	Z	Z	Z	—	—	X	X
D	X	—	—	Z	Z	Z	Z	X	X	X	O	O	O	O	X	X	X	Z	Z	Z	Z	—	—	X

→ → → → → → → → → → → → ← ← ← ← ← ← ← ← ← ← ← ←

X = 42 = purple   Z = 32 = magenta

— = 16 = off white (lighter weight)   O = 6 = light orange (lighter weight)

Figure 104. A band woven from Pattern Draft 4. Two weights of wool, 3″ wide, draft and weaving by Julia Bauder. The designs result not only from regular four forward, four backward rotation of the cards, but also from turning the entire deck of cards simultaneously, but out of the regular sequence. In some areas cards have been picked up and rearranged in the deck (see Chapter 7).

Figure 105. Pattern Draft 5.

	1	2	3	4	5	6	7	8	9	10	11	12	13	14	15
A	X	Z	Z	X	Z	Z	X	O	X	Z	Z	X	Z	Z	X
B	X	Z	X	X	X	Z	X	O	X	Z	X	X	X	Z	X
C	X	Z	Z	Z	Z	Z	X	O	X	Z	Z	Z	Z	Z	X
D	X	—	—	Z	—	—	X	O	X	—	—	Z	—	—	X

→ → → → → → → → ← ← ← ← ← ← ←

Z = 24 = olive

X = 24 = yellow green

— = 8 = yellow

O = 4 = brown (heavier)

Figure 106. A band woven from Pattern Draft 5. A 3-ply rug wool was used for the "O" strands (the middle stripe) and a lighter weight acrylic yarn was used for the rest of the band. The band is 1¼" wide, draft and weaving by Kenneth Storey. The entire belt was worked in the usual sequence of four turns toward and four away.

Figure 107. Pattern Draft 6.

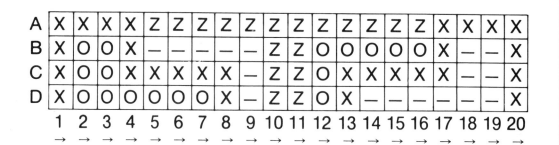

	1	2	3	4	5	6	7	8	9	10	11	12	13	14	15	16	17	18	19	20
A	X	X	X	X	Z	Z	Z	Z	Z	Z	Z	Z	Z	Z	Z	X	X	X	X	X
B	X	O	O	X	–	–	–	–	–	Z	Z	O	O	O	O	O	X	–	–	X
C	X	O	O	X	X	X	X	X	–	Z	Z	O	X	X	X	X	X	–	–	X
D	X	O	O	O	O	O	O	X	–	Z	Z	O	X	–	–	–	–	–	–	X

→ → → → → → → → → → → → → → → → → → → →

X = 28 = dark brown

O = 17 = gold

– = 17 = orange

Z = 18 = green

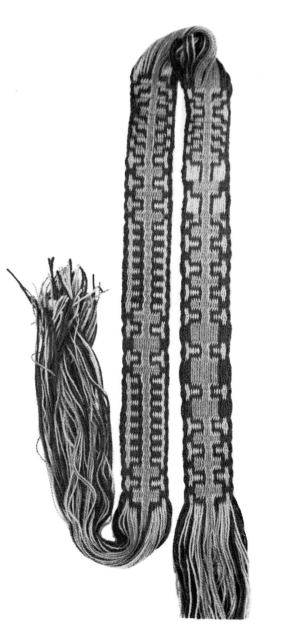

Figure 108. *A band woven from Pattern Draft 6. A combination of 2- and 3-ply wool rug yarn, 2½" wide, draft and weaving by Joyce Arata. The weaving began on the right, turning four turns toward and four away, to provide a series of box shapes. The larger boxes were made by turning four turns toward the body, then one away, then one toward to extend the box. (This creates float threads with a woven inner layer as described in Chapter 6.) The box is closed by weaving four turns away. Other sections were woven by turning the cards in one direction or by sequences involving two turns toward and two turns away.*

Figure 109. Pattern Draft 7.

	1	2	3	4	5	6	7	8	9	10	11	12	13	14	15	16	17	18	19	20
A	X	X	X	X	O	O	O	O	O	O	O	O	O	O	O	O	O	X	X	X
B	X	O	O	X	O	O	X	X	X	O	O	X	X	X	O	O	X	O	O	X
C	X	O	O	X	X	X	X	O	X	O	O	X	O	X	X	X	X	O	O	X
D	X	O	O	O	O	O	O	O	X	O	O	X	O	O	O	O	O	O	O	X

→ → → → → → → → → → → → → → → → → → → →

$X = 34 = black$

$O = 46 = natural$

Figure 110. *A band woven from Pattern Draft 7. Natural, 2-ply, roughly spun goat hair, and a single-ply combination of horse hair and human hair, 4" wide. The draft is by Diane Dowling and the weaving is by the author. The heavy, coarse materials cause the pattern to be spread-out and wide. The indistinctness in the pattern is caused by the dark (warp) threads being of a lighter weight. The tassels, attached to four-strand braids, were laid in during the weaving (see Chapter 7). The cards were turned four turns toward and four away.*

Figure 111. *The back panel of a wool cape, each strip 3½″ wide, drafts and weaving by the author. The three strips on the right were woven from Pattern Drafts 8, 9, and 10. They were worked primarily by turning four turns toward and four away, but some sections have the cards turning continuously in one direction.*

Figure 112. Pattern Draft 8.

	1	2	3	4	5	6	7	8	9	10	11	12	13	14	15	16	17	18	19	20	21	22	23	24
A	X	X	X	X	X	O	Z	P	P	P	P	P	S	M	—	—	—	W	O	X	X	X	X	X
B	X	X	X	X	O	O	Z	P	P	P	P	P	S	M	—	—	—	W	O	O	X	X	X	X
C	X	X	X	O	O	—	Z	Z	Z	Z	Z	Z	S	M	W	W	W	W	—	O	O	X	X	X
D	X	X	O	O	—	—	—	—	—	—	—	—	S	M	—	—	—	—	—	—	O	O	X	X

→ → → → → → → → → → → → → ← ← ← ← ← ← ← ← ← ← ←

$X = 28 = blue$ $S = 4 = red\ (bright)$

$O = 14 = orange$ $M = 4 = pink$

$— = 22 = brown$ $W = 6 = purple$

$P = 10 = green$ $Z = 8 = burgundy\ (dark\ red)$

Figure 113. Pattern Draft 9.

	1	2	3	4	5	6	7	8	9	10	11	12	13	14	15	16	17	18	19	20	21	22	23	24
A	X	X	O	O	S	S	X	X	P	P	—	Z	Z	—	P	P	X	X	S	S	O	O	X	X
B	X	X	O	S	S	X	X	P	P	—	—	Z	Z	—	—	P	P	X	X	S	S	O	X	X
C	X	X	S	S	X	X	P	P	—	—	Z	Z	Z	Z	—	—	P	P	X	X	S	S	X	X
D	X	X	S	X	X	P	P	—	—	Z	Z	O	O	Z	Z	—	—	P	P	X	X	S	X	X

→ → → → → → → → → → → → ← ← ← ← ← ← ← ← ← ← ← ←

$X = 32 = blue$ $P = 16 = pink$

$O = 8 = green$ $— = 14 = purple$

$S = 14 = brown$ $Z = 12 = orange$

Figure 114. Pattern Draft 10.

	1	2	3	4	5	6	7	8	9	10	11	12	13	14	15	16	17	18	19	20	21	22	23	24
A	X	X	X	O	O	—	W	W	W	P	S	P	P	S	P	W	W	W	—	O	O	X	X	X
B	X	X	O	O	—	W	W	W	P	S	P	Z	Z	P	S	P	W	W	W	—	O	O	X	X
C	X	O	O	—	W	W	W	P	S	P	Z	P	P	Z	P	S	P	W	W	W	—	O	O	X
D	X	O	—	W	W	W	P	S	P	Z	P	Z	Z	P	Z	P	S	P	W	W	W	—	O	X

→ → → → → → → → → → → → ← ← ← ← ← ← ← ← ← ← ← ←

$X = 14 = burgundy\ (dark\ red)$ $P = 20 = orange$

$— = 8 = pink$ $S = 8 = brown$

$W = 24 = purple$ $Z = 8 = green$

Figure 115. Pattern Draft 11.

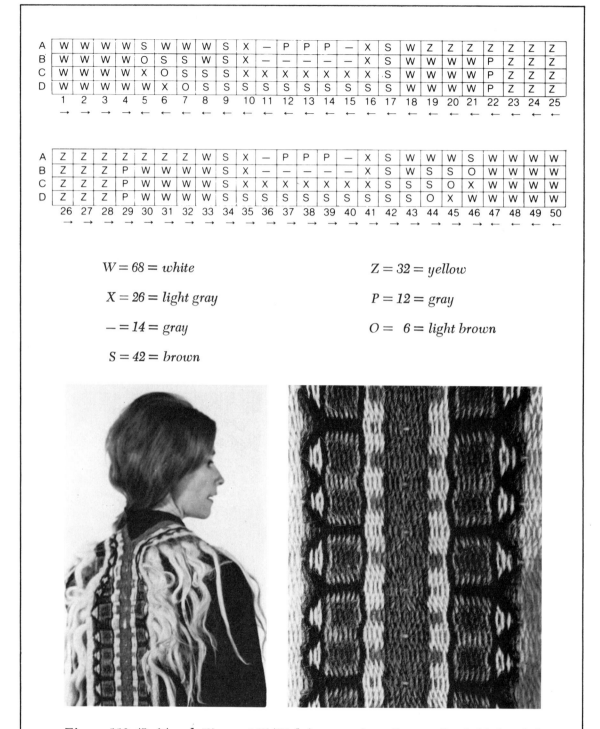

	1	2	3	4	5	6	7	8	9	10	11	12	13	14	15	16	17	18	19	20	21	22	23	24	25
A	W	W	W	W	S	W	W	W	S	X	—	P	P	P	—	X	S	W	Z	Z	Z	Z	Z	Z	Z
B	W	W	W	W	O	S	S	W	S	X	—	—	—	—	—	X	S	W	W	W	W	W	P	Z	Z
C	W	W	W	W	X	O	S	S	S	X	X	X	X	X	X	X	S	W	W	W	W	W	P	Z	Z
D	W	W	W	W	W	X	O	S	S	S	S	S	S	S	S	S	S	W	W	W	W	W	P	Z	Z
	→	→	→	→	←	←	←	←	←	←	←	←	←	←	←	←	←	←	←	←	←	←	←	←	←

	26	27	28	29	30	31	32	33	34	35	36	37	38	39	40	41	42	43	44	45	46	47	48	49	50
A	Z	Z	Z	Z	Z	Z	Z	W	S	X	—	P	P	P	—	X	S	W	W	W	S	W	W	W	W
B	Z	Z	Z	P	W	W	W	W	S	X	—	—	—	—	—	X	S	W	S	S	O	W	W	W	W
C	Z	Z	Z	P	W	W	W	W	S	X	X	X	X	X	X	X	S	S	S	O	X	W	W	W	W
D	Z	Z	Z	P	W	W	W	W	S	S	S	S	S	S	S	S	S	S	S	O	X	W	W	W	W
	→	→	→	→	→	→	→	→	→	→	→	→	→	→	→	→	→	→	→	→	→	←	←	←	←

$W = 68 =$ white $Z = 32 =$ yellow

$X = 26 =$ light gray $P = 12 =$ gray

$— = 14 =$ gray $O = 6 =$ light brown

$S = 42 =$ brown

Figure 116 (Left) and **Figure 117** (Right) woven from Pattern Draft 11. Swedish yarns in natural colors combined with long locks of sheep's wool, 7″ wide, draft and weaving by the author. The pattern was done in the four turns toward, four away sequence, with occasionally only three turns toward and three away. This omits the dark bar in the design and is shown clearly in the detail in Figure 117.

Figure 118. Pattern Draft 12.

	1	2	3	4	5	6	7	8	9	10	11
A	X	X	—	O	O	O	O	O	O	O	X
B	X	X	X	—	O	—	O	O	O	O	X
C	X	X	X	X	—	X	—	O	O	O	X
D	X	X	X	X	X	X	X	—	O	O	X

← ← ← ← ← ← ← ← ← ← →

X = 21 = *dark blue*

— = 6 = *white*

O = 17 = *red*

Figure 119. *A band woven from Pattern Draft 12. Plied-wool yarn, 1″ wide, draft and weaving by Bettie Adams. The band was woven normally, four turns toward the body and four away.*

Figure 120. Pattern Draft 13.

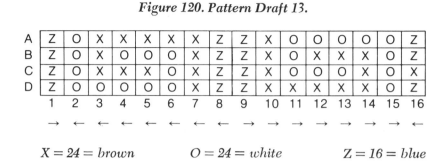

	1	2	3	4	5	6	7	8	9	10	11	12	13	14	15	16
A	Z	O	X	X	X	X	X	Z	Z	X	O	O	O	O	O	Z
B	Z	O	X	O	O	O	X	Z	Z	X	O	X	X	X	O	Z
C	Z	O	X	X	X	O	X	Z	Z	X	O	O	O	X	O	X
D	Z	O	O	O	O	O	X	Z	Z	X	X	X	X	X	O	Z

→ ← ← ← ← ← ← ← → → → → → → → ←

X = 24 = brown   O = 24 = white   Z = 16 = blue

Figure 121. Pattern Draft 14.

	1	2	3	4	5	6	7	8	9	10	11	12
A	Z	Z	X	X	X	Z	X	X	Z	O	O	Z
B	Z	Z	X	Z	Z	Z	Z	Z	Z	O	O	Z
C	Z	Z	X	O	O	O	O	O	Z	O	O	Z
D	Z	Z	X	O	O	Z	O	O	Z	O	O	Z
E	Z	Z	X	O	O	Z	Z	Z	Z	O	O	Z
F	Z	Z	X	O	O	O	O	O	O	O	O	Z

← ← → → → → → → → → → ←

X = 10 = red   O = 29 = white   Z = 33 = brown

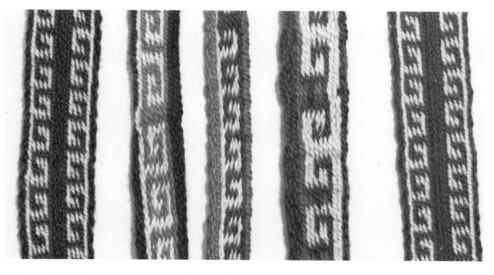

Figure 122. *Five bands woven from Pattern Drafts 13 and 14. Plied Swedish wool yarn, ¾″ to 1″ wide, drafts and weaving by Bettie Adams. The two outside bands were woven from Pattern Draft 13. The cards were turned continuously in one direction and reversed only when the warp threads became too twisted to continue. Pattern Draft 14 is similar, but designed for six-holed cards, and is shown in the second band from the right. The cards were turned six turns toward the body and six turns away.*

Figure 123. Pattern Draft 15.

	1	2	3	4	5	6	7	8	9	10	11	12	13	14	15	16	17	18	19	20
A	X	X	X	X	—	Z	P	—	—	X	O	O	—	—	—	—	—	—	P	P
B	X	X	X	—	—	—	Z	P	—	O	X	X	—	—	—	—	—	P	P	P
C	X	P	P	X	—	—	—	Z	P	—	O	O	X	X	Z	Z	Z	P	—	—
D	X	Z	Z	P	X	—	—	—	Z	P	—	O	X	X	X	Z	Z	Z	Z	Z
E	X	P	P	X	—	—	—	Z	P	—	—	O	O	O	X	X	X	X	X	X
F	X	X	X	—	—	—	—	—	Z	P	—	—	—	—	—	O	O	O	O	O

← ← ← ← ← ← ← ← ← ← ← ← ← ← ← ← ← ← ← ←

	21	22	23	24	25	26	27	28	29	30	31	32	33	34	35	36	37	38	39	40	41
A	P	P	P	—	—	—	—	—	—	O	O	X	—	—	P	Z	—	X	X	X	X
B	Z	P	P	P	—	—	—	—	—	X	X	O	—	P	Z	—	—	—	X	X	X
C	—	—	—	P	Z	Z	Z	X	X	O	O	—	P	Z	—	—	—	X	P	P	X
D	—	Z	Z	Z	Z	Z	X	X	X	O	—	P	Z	—	—	—	X	P	Z	Z	X
E	—	X	X	X	X	X	O	O	O	—	—	P	Z	—	—	—	—	X	P	P	X
F	X	O	O	O	O	O	—	—	—	—	—	P	Z	—	—	—	—	—	X	X	X

→ →

X = 28 = *purple*

O = 59 = *plum*

2 = 33 = *pink*

P = 35 = *orange*

— = 91 = *white*

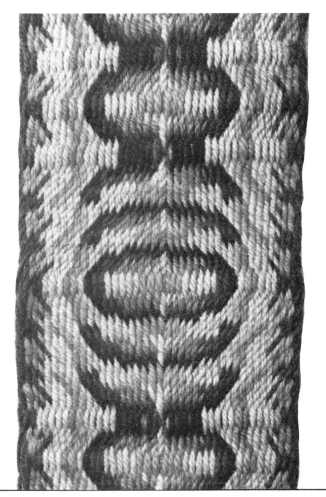

Figure 124. A band woven from Pattern Draft 15, using six-holed cards. Wool, 3-ply rug yarn, 4½″ wide, draft and weaving by Susan Boblitt. The band was woven by turning six turns toward the body and six turns away, except for the center section, which was eighteen turns toward and eighteen turns away.

Figure 125. Pattern Draft 16.

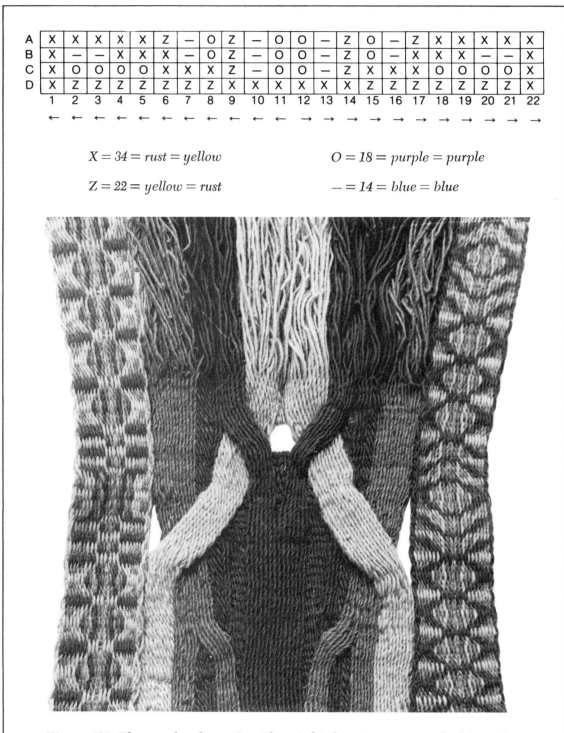

	1	2	3	4	5	6	7	8	9	10	11	12	13	14	15	16	17	18	19	20	21	22
A	X	X	X	X	X	Z	–	O	Z	–	O	O	–	Z	O	–	Z	X	X	X	X	X
B	X	–	–	X	X	X	–	O	Z	–	O	O	–	Z	O	–	X	X	X	–	–	X
C	X	O	O	O	O	X	X	X	Z	–	O	O	–	Z	X	X	X	O	O	O	O	X
D	X	Z	Z	Z	Z	Z	Z	Z	X	X	X	X	X	X	X	Z	Z	Z	Z	Z	Z	X

← ← ← ← ← ← ← ← ← ← ← → → → → → → → → → → →

X = 34 = rust = yellow   O = 18 = purple = purple

Z = 22 = yellow = rust   − = 14 = blue = blue

Figure 126. *The two bands on the sides of this hanging were worked from Pattern Draft 16. Single-ply Swedish wool yarn, each 2″ wide, draft and weaving by Janet Bucknam. In the left-hand band, X-yellow; in the right-hand band, X-rust. Both were woven in the four turns toward and four away sequence, except in the middle, which is twelve turns toward and twelve away.*

Figure 127. Pattern Draft 17.

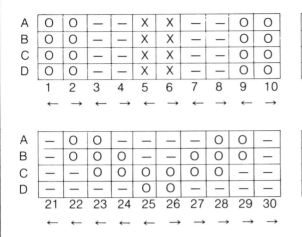

	1	2	3	4	5	6	7	8	9	10
A	O	O	—	—	X	X	—	—	O	O
B	O	O	—	—	X	X	—	—	O	O
C	O	O	—	—	X	X	—	—	O	O
D	O	O	—	—	X	X	—	—	O	O

← → ← → ← → ← → ← →

	11	12	13	14	15	16	17	18	19	20
A	—	O	O	—	—	—	—	O	O	—
B	—	O	O	O	—	—	O	O	O	—
C	—	—	O	O	O	O	O	O	—	—
D	—	—	—	—	O	O	—	—	—	—

← ← ← ← ← → → → → →

	21	22	23	24	25	26	27	28	29	30
A	—	O	O	—	—	—	—	O	O	—
B	—	O	O	O	—	—	O	O	O	—
C	—	—	O	O	O	O	O	O	—	—
D	—	—	—	—	O	O	—	—	—	—

← ← ← ← ← → → → → →

	31	32	33	34	35	36	37	38	39	40
A	O	O	—	—	X	X	—	—	O	O
B	O	O	—	—	X	X	—	—	O	O
C	O	O	—	—	X	X	—	—	O	O
D	O	O	—	—	X	X	—	—	O	O

← → ← → ← → ← → ← →

$X = 16 = blue$

$O = 68 = brown$

$— = 76 = white$

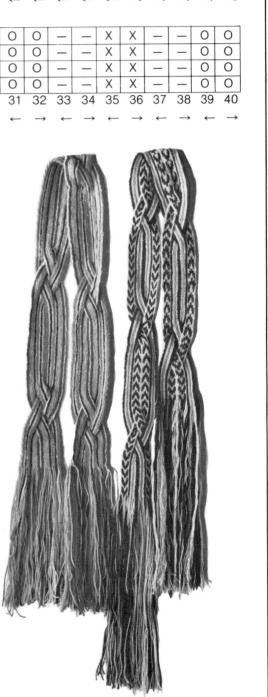

Figure 128. Two wool bands, each woven in four 10-card sections, each 3″ wide, draft and weaving by Bettie Adams. The band on the left was woven in horizontal stripes, while the band on the right was woven from Pattern Draft 17. The sections have been woven individually, then crossed to form a braided effect. The 40 cards were set up together in sets of 10 cards each. In the beginning all the cards were worked together and turned twelve turns toward the weaver's body. The four groups were then split up and woven with individual weft threads, twelve turns toward, then twelve away. The separated sections were braided together by moving the groups of cards laterally. Weaving with a single weft thread was then resumed and the cards were turned twenty-eight turns away before the next split.

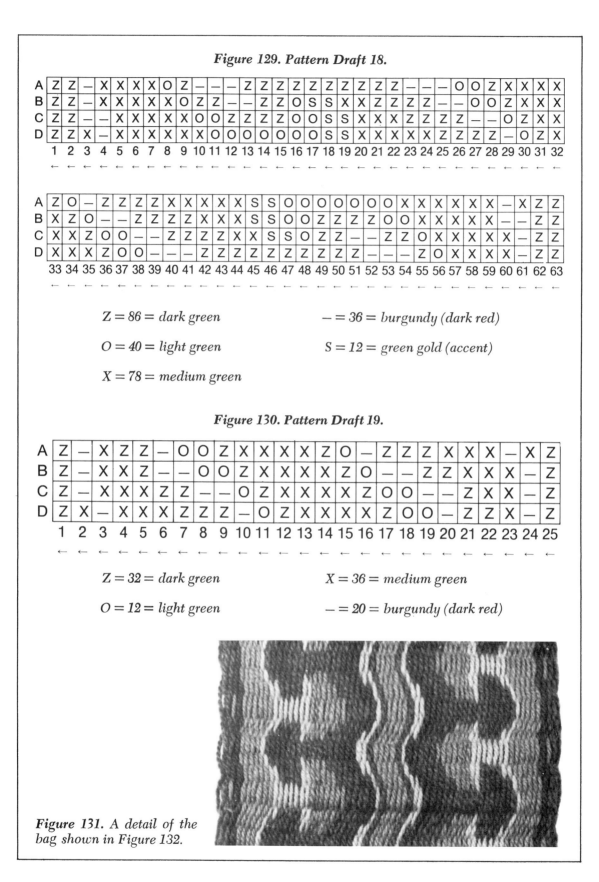

Figure 129. Pattern Draft 18.

	1	2	3	4	5	6	7	8	9	10	11	12	13	14	15	16	17	18	19	20	21	22	23	24	25	26	27	28	29	30	31	32
A	Z	Z	–	X	X	X	X	O	Z	–	–	–	Z	Z	Z	Z	Z	Z	Z	Z	Z	Z	–	–	–	O	O	Z	X	X	X	X
B	Z	Z	–	X	X	X	X	O	Z	Z	–	–	Z	Z	O	S	S	X	X	Z	Z	Z	Z	–	–	O	O	Z	X	X	X	
C	Z	Z	–	–	X	X	X	X	O	O	Z	Z	Z	O	O	S	S	X	X	X	Z	Z	Z	Z	–	–	O	Z	X	X		
D	Z	Z	X	–	X	X	X	X	X	O	O	O	O	O	O	O	O	S	S	X	X	X	X	X	Z	Z	Z	Z	–	O	Z	X

← ← ← ← ← ← ← ← ← ← ← ← ← ← ← ←

	33	34	35	36	37	38	39	40	41	42	43	44	45	46	47	48	49	50	51	52	53	54	55	56	57	58	59	60	61	62	63
A	Z	O	–	Z	Z	Z	X	X	X	X	X	S	S	O	O	O	O	O	O	O	O	X	X	X	X	X	X	–	X	Z	Z
B	X	Z	O	–	–	Z	Z	Z	X	X	X	S	S	O	O	Z	Z	Z	Z	O	O	X	X	X	X	–	–	–	Z	Z	
C	X	X	Z	O	O	–	–	Z	Z	Z	Z	X	S	S	O	Z	Z	–	–	Z	Z	O	X	X	X	X	–	–	Z	Z	
D	X	X	X	Z	O	O	–	–	–	Z	Z	Z	Z	Z	Z	Z	Z	–	–	–	Z	O	X	X	X	X	–	–	Z	Z	

← ← ← ← ← ← ← ← ← ← ← ← ← ← ← ← ←

Z = 86 = dark green   − = 36 = burgundy (dark red)

O = 40 = light green   S = 12 = green gold (accent)

X = 78 = medium green

Figure 130. Pattern Draft 19.

	1	2	3	4	5	6	7	8	9	10	11	12	13	14	15	16	17	18	19	20	21	22	23	24	25
A	Z	–	X	Z	Z	–	O	O	Z	X	X	X	X	Z	O	–	Z	Z	Z	X	X	X	–	X	Z
B	Z	–	X	X	Z	–	–	O	O	Z	X	X	X	X	Z	O	–	–	Z	Z	X	X	X	–	Z
C	Z	–	X	X	Z	Z	–	–	O	Z	X	X	X	X	Z	O	O	–	–	Z	X	X	–	Z	
D	Z	X	–	X	X	X	Z	Z	Z	–	O	Z	X	X	X	X	Z	O	O	–	Z	Z	X	–	Z

← ←

Z = 32 = dark green   X = 36 = medium green

O = 12 = light green   − = 20 = burgundy (dark red)

Figure 131. A detail of the bag shown in Figure 132.

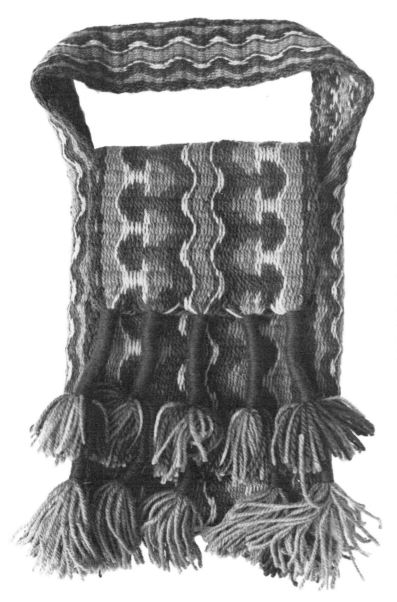

Figure 132. The body of this bag, woven in 3-ply rug yarn, 7″ wide, followed Pattern Draft 18; the handle, 2¼″ wide, followed Pattern Draft 19. The bag was stitched together and has wrapped fringe. The turning sequence was four turns toward and four turns away. The pattern and weaving are by Roxanne Clarke, based on a pattern from Byways in Handweaving by Mary Atwater.

Figure 133. Pattern Draft 20.

	1	2	3	4	5	6	7	8	9	10	11	12	13	14	15	16	17	18
A	X	X	X	X	+	+	+	+	X	X	+	+	+	+	X	X	X	X
B	X	X	X	X	X	+	+	X	X	X	X	+	+	X	X	X	X	X
C	X	X	+	+	X	X	X	X	+	+	X	X	X	X	+	+	X	X
D	X	X	+	+	+	X	X	+	+	+	+	X	X	+	+	+	X	X
	←	←	←	←	←	←	→	→	→	→	←	←	←	→	→	→	→	→

X = 44 = any color

This pattern is an example of the skip-hole technique, using one color. The holes represented by blank spaces are not threaded and these card holes remain empty during weaving. This causes depressions in the woven surface and exposure of the weft thread.

6. THE DOUBLE WEAVE AND ITS VARIATIONS

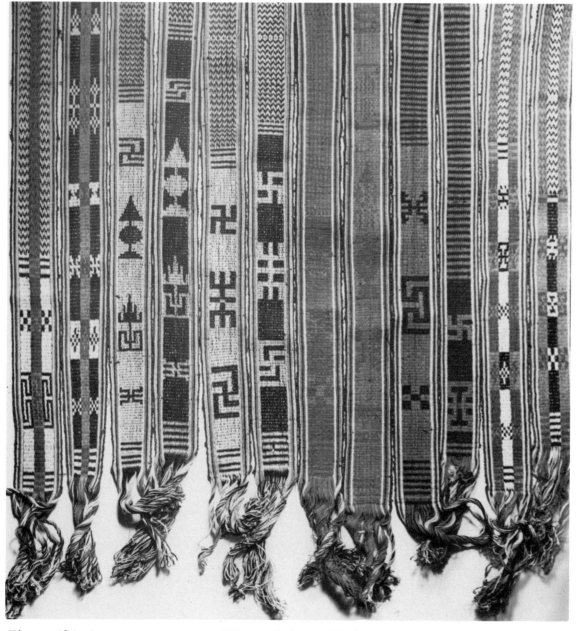

Figure 134. Contemporary cotton Tibetan belts, with designs woven in the double-face technique.

Double weaving, the simultaneous weaving of two separate layers of fabric (as well as variations on the double weave), can be done along with regular card weaving and requires no special threading or setting up.

The methods described in this chapter will be much clearer if you thread 10 or more cards according to the pattern draft given in Figure 135. The directions for each of the four techniques discussed here may be worked out on a sample belt, and each step will be discussed in reference to this specific sample. Begin the sample with several rows of regular weave (four turns toward you, four turns away), and separate each experimental section with a similar stretch of regular weaving. Smooth, medium-weight plied yarn is best for this first double weave sampler. Warp strands should be in two colors, one light and one dark. This will give you a clear and distinct definition of the position and layers of threads.

The instructions in this chapter are for the weaving set up with the cards facing the left. Once the principles are clear, the weaver can discover and develop variations on each of the techniques presented, with little to limit the ways they can be used, combined, and developed.

Double Weaving

With the double weave technique you can weave words, messages, tubes, and pockets into a card weaving. Double weave can enrich and add dimension to a card weaving design because the thickness of the two simultaneously woven layers is very lush and full.

Begin the sample belt by weaving four turns toward your body and four turns away. Horizontal stripes will appear if you alternate dark and light.

Now begin the double weave section by holding the cards in the position shown in Figure 136, #1, with the A holes, carrying dark threads, on the top. Move the cards back and forth until two clear sheds appear. Pass the weft thread through the top shed, around the edge, and back through the bottom shed. The weft thread will have made a "circle," passing through the top shed, then back through the bottom shed. Now rock the cards and bring the B holes to the top (Figure 136, #2). Clear the shed and bring the weft thread again through the top, around the edge, and across the bottom, making the circle again.

Continue weaving in this manner, alternating between holes A and B in the top position. Two individual woven layers will be formed, the top dark and the bottom light, joined along both sides. Any combination of two holes alternated in this way can be used, depending on what color the weaver wants on the top layer.

Many interesting bands can be woven working the dark threads on top then rotating the cards to put light threads on the top. These areas can then be stuffed to give emphasis and depth. The tubes formed this way are closed up as soon as a new combination of holes is brought to the top, whether it's by rotating the cards or by going back to normal weaving. Words, inscriptions, and designs are formed by double weaving with dark threads on the surface and then turning individual cards half-way around

A	X	X	X	X	X	X	X	X	X	X
B	X	X	X	X	X	X	X	X	X	X
C	O	O	O	O	O	O	O	O	O	O
D	O	O	O	O	O	O	O	O	O	O
	1	2	3	4	5	6	7	8	9	10

→ → → → → → → → → →

Figure 135. *A pattern for setting up a double-weave sampler. The X's represent dark threads, while the O's represent light-colored threads. You may use 10 or more cards.*

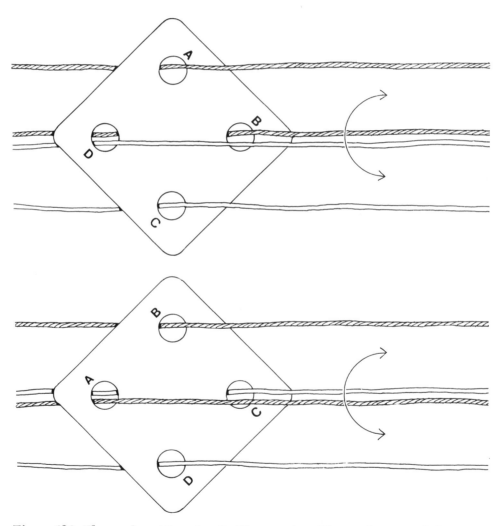

Figure 136. *The card positions for double weaving. The cards are angled to form two weaving sheds and are rocked back and forth between any two holes (in this case between A and B, putting dark threads on the top). In order to maintain two individual and separate layers of weaving, the same two holes must be used continuously. After each card shift the weft thread goes through both sheds, as indicated by the arrows. The weaving produced will have two separate layers.*

Figure 137. *A linen sash, 3½" wide, by the author. The sash used 50 cards, and the date was worked in the double-weave technique.*

Figure 138. *A partially woven band, medium-weight 3-ply wool yarn, by the author. The word was done in the double-weave technique.*

Figure 139. *A double-woven scarf in 3-ply wool, 4" wide, by the author. Except along the extreme borders, the color and design on the back of the weaving are the exact reverse of what appears on the top surface.*

(two quarter-turns) so that light threads appear where dark threads were. Where cards are so individually turned, white threads will appear on the weaving surface and black on the bottom. Each time cards are turned to bring different holes to the top the two layers of weaving are joined.

Designs can be carefully worked out on graph paper or done spontaneously as the weaving progresses. The handling of the weft thread will, for the most part, determine how the weaving will turn out. If one weft thread (as described) is used going across the top and then across the bottom shed of the weaving, two layers will be formed that are joined on the edges. In order to form two separate layers that aren't attached on either edge, two weft threads can be used, one going back and forth through the top shed, the other going back and forth through the bottom shed.

By experimenting with the ways the weft thread may be handled, the weaver can produce two layers free of one another or joined in many different ways. Open or secret pockets, flaps of many kinds, slits, stuffed or empty tubes, "printed" messages, all can be made with ease using the double weave technique.

Double-Face Weaving

Double-face weaving produces a surface similar to that created with the double weave, but it's woven with a normal shed, and produces just one, not two, separate layers of woven fabric. It can produce one color on the top and one on the bottom, so that designs and inscriptions can be woven in. Double weaving produces a tighter, neater design, but double-face weaving is considerably easier, and the fabric it produces isn't as thick. The series of illustrations in Figure 140 shows the card positions for a double-face weaving. In these illustrations, and for your own convenience in weaving a sample, card holes A and B carry dark threads, which will show on the surface of the weaving.

The weaving process is much like that used in regular weave, with a full open shed, and a weft thread that moves as it would in regular weaving. To begin the double-face weaving sample, place holes A and B, with the dark surface threads, on the far side of the deck of cards (Figure 140, #1). Bring the weft thread through the shed, turn the cards one quarter-turn toward you to bring holes A and B to the top (Figure 140, #2), and bring the weft thread through the shed again.

Now turn the cards so holes A and B are toward your body (Figure 140, #3), and bring the weft thread through the new shed. Repeat the sequence backwards by bringing holes A and B to the top again, and then to the far side, passing the weft thread through each shed as it's formed. The top surface of the weaving will be dark, the bottom white. Letters and designs may be created by turning individual cards half-way around so that light threads show where the dark threads were.

Double-face weaving can be effective when used with patterns. It can be used to extend or elongate a design within a regular card weaving, and it can also be used to foreshorten or telescope such designs. Any two holes

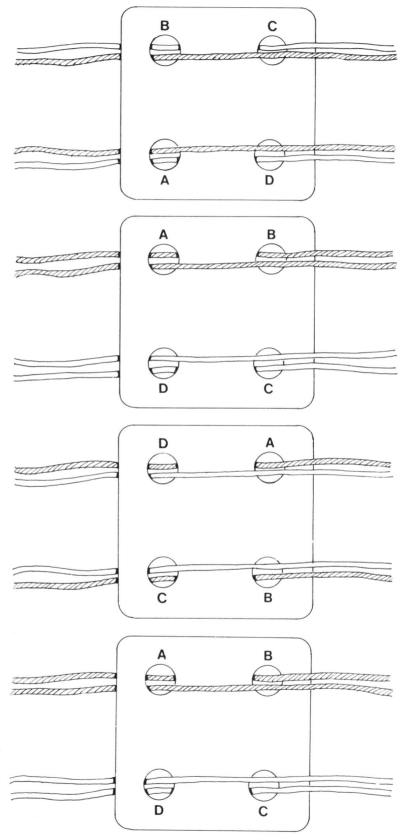

Figure 140. In double-face weaving, sequences of three quarter-turns are used rather than the usual four. In this example only the threads going through holes A and B (dark) will show on the surface of the weaving.

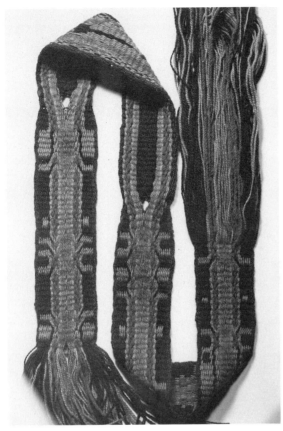

Figure 141. *A wool hanging, 3" wide, by Ana Lisa Hedstrom. Sections of the pattern have been elongated by alternating double-face weaving with regular weaving. Cards have been moved laterally during weaving to create layers and shifts in pattern.*

Figure 142. *A contemporary cotton Tibetan belt, 2" wide, with designs at each end woven in the double-face technique.*

Figure 143. *A belt of 4-ply wool yarn, 3" wide, by Hilda Rasmussen. On the upper left of the weaving float threads extend parts of the pattern, making large, bold designs.*

may be worked, such as A and B are in Figure 140. The threads going through the holes that follow this pattern of movement will always appear on the surface of the weaving.

Weaving with Floating Warp Threads

Warp threads that "float" over a woven area can affect the texture and design of a card weaving. Used primarily in wall hangings or other non-functional weavings, floating threads tend to shape and elongate the design, and to create linear texture in the woven surface. This technique can be used either with the double weave technique or with regular (or plain) card weaving.

In double weave, floating threads are created by passing a weft thread through the shed of just one of the layers being woven. The layer in which no weft thread is being worked will appear as unbound, floating warp threads. As soon as normal weaving is resumed these floating warp threads again become part of the regular weaving.

In regular weave, floating threads appear both above and under the layer of woven fabric, which is sandwiched between the two layers of floating threads. If, for instance, you want the threads that go through the A holes to float on the top surface, begin with a normal weaving shed, with holes A and B on the top (Figure 140, #2) and bring the weft thread across. Now turn the cards one-quarter turn toward your body, so that holes D and A are on top (Figure 140, #3), and bring the weft thread back again through the shed. Next, turn the cards one-quarter turn back, so that holes A and B are on top, and again bring the weft thread across.

Figure 144. A wool, mohair, and alpaca belt, 2" wide, by Ana Lisa Hedstrom. This belt was fashioned after the love tokens of bygone days, and the message was worked in the double-face technique.

Continue weaving in this sequence, with hole A always one of the two holes on top, and hole C always one of the two holes on the bottom. These A and C threads will not be woven in, since the weft thread will bind only the warp threads that pass through holes B and D. When you return to normal weaving (four turns toward you, four turns away) the floating threads will work back into the weaving.

Tubular Weaving

Although it's possible to form a tube by double weaving, the phrase "tubular weaving" refers specifically to a tube formed by drawing together the two edges of a band woven in the regular weave. To create a tubular card weaving, begin normally with a plain shed and pass the weft thread through from right to left. On the next turn of the cards *do not* bring the weft thread back across through the shed from the left, but instead carry the weft thread underneath the weaving, insert it again from the right, and again pull it out from the left side (Figure 146).

A tubular shape will exist as long as the weft thread is inserted, brought under the weaving, and (after each turn of the cards) again passed through the shed from the same direction. The actual tube will be formed when the weft thread is pulled tight enough to bring the two edges of the weaving together. With rough or fuzzy threads the tube should be formed soon after each weft passage, while with very smooth thread the weft may be pulled tight after several turns of the cards.

Figure 145. *Woolen band, 2½″ wide, by Lorraine Herald. The pattern has been broken by sections of float threads on the surface. Wrapped circular pieces were added to hold the float threads aside, causing the bottom layer to pop through.*

Figure 146. Detail of woolen hanging, 6½" wide, by Liz Brierley. The long, thin areas that join the weaving to the wood were woven in the tubular technique.

7. FINISHING

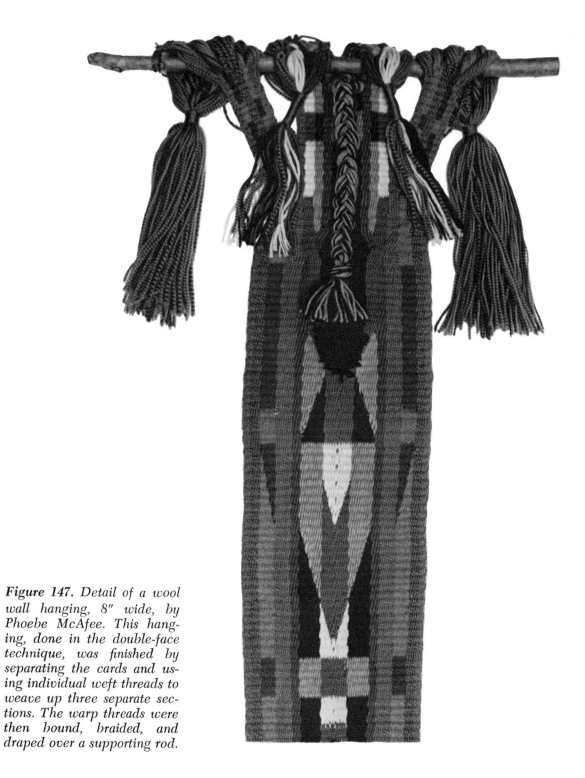

Figure 147. *Detail of a wool wall hanging, 8″ wide, by Phoebe McAfee. This hanging, done in the double-face technique, was finished by separating the cards and using individual weft threads to weave up three separate sections. The warp threads were then bound, braided, and draped over a supporting rod.*

Card weavings, because of their tightness and intertwined density, are essentially finished when the cards are slipped off and the fringe is trimmed. However, a number of special techniques, most of them quite ancient, can add texture, beauty, and richness to the completed weaving. Many different ideas for incorporating dowels, sticks, and supports for wall hangings are illustrated in photographs throughout this book. Specific instructions for wrapping, braiding, twisting, and knotting are given in this chapter, along with directions for making tassels, adding beads during weaving, making fringes, and decreasing warp threads. These techniques may be combined or developed further, with no real limit to their use.

Using Individual Card-woven Bands

The prime characteristics of card weavings produced through the ages have been their strength, pliability, and durability. These weavings for the most part were narrow bands used as reins, bridles, saddle girths, belts, straps, and all manner of trim. Their rich and decorative patterns, their strength and durability, and their very special "feel" make card-woven bands ideal for such things as garment trims, headbands, sandal straps, ropes, guitar and camera straps, bands to hold flowerpots, swings, and shoulder bags. Card-woven bands can also be used with wood, leather, fabric, and ceramics. Individual bands can be doubled over or woven with slits to form neck pieces. Many contemporary card weavers use the technique for producing wide bands that have little practical value, but serve as decorative belts or hangings.

Wrapping

The thick, full warp end fringes of card weaving can often be enhanced by wrapping or binding. Figure 154 shows a group of threads being wrapped. In the method illustrated, which is best for short wrappings, one end of the wrapping material is formed into a loop and placed on top of the parallel threads to be wrapped.

The wrapping proceeds toward the closed end of the loop until the area to be covered is bound. The wrapping thread is then cut, and the end is inserted through the loop. Each of the two free ends is pulled away from the other with strong, even pressure until the loop is brought back snugly under the tightly bound wrapped section. The ends can then be cut flush.

If a much larger area is to be wrapped, one end of the wrapping thread can be placed on top of the parallel threads, then bound tightly as the wrapping process proceeds. When about 2″ of wrapping is left to do, a separate piece of yarn about 6″ to 8″ long is doubled and bound into the wrapping with its loop protruding, very much as in the first method (see Figure 154). The end of the wrapping thread is then cut, placed in the loop, and withdrawn back under the wrapped section as the loop is pulled under those threads that had bound it. The loop thread is then discarded, and the end of the wrapping thread, if it protrudes, is trimmed. Still an-

Figure 148. *Plied-wool belt with ceramic beads and partially wrapped fringe, 3″ wide, by Toni Horgos.*

Figure 149. *Fine, plied-wool belt, 2½″ wide, by Robert Cranford.*

Figure 150. *Plied-wool belt laced through three buckles, 2″ wide, by Irene Conley.*

Figure 151. *Plied-wool belt with a horn buckle, 3″ wide, by Jack Dunstan.*

Figure 152. *Sample Band A, woven in wool with feathers, beads, and wood, 1½″ wide, by Carol Krieg.*

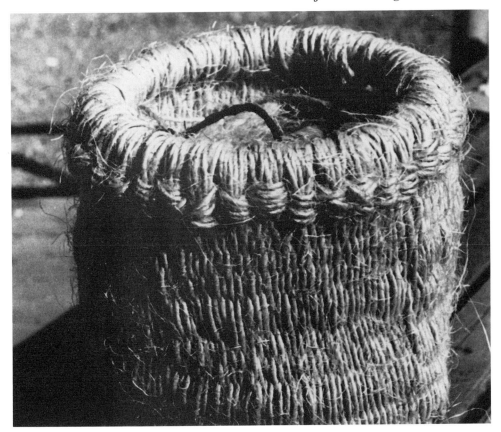

Figure 153. *A sisal basket made from a card-woven band and an embroidery hoop by Maria Elena Arejula. Photograph by Kathy McCardle.*

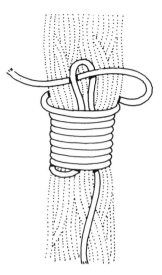

Figure 154. Wrapping or binding groups of threads.

Figure 155. Detail of wool neckpiece, 6″ wide, by Marie Backs. Long areas of fringe were wrapped in different colors.

other method is to use a heavy tapestry needle to work in the ends of the wrapping material. This is a simple method but it is more difficult to get a permanently tight wrapping this way. In any of these methods, extra threads can be wrapped in to make heavier fringes, or to add new colors. Wire can be bound in to make the wrapped area stiff and easily formed.

Four-Strand Braiding

Many kinds of braiding are popular for finishing and controlling fringes. Common three-strand braiding offers an attractive flat braid, and four-strand braiding results in a strong round braid. The placement of color strongly affects the pattern of the four-strand braid, which can be worked from either four individual threads, or from four groups of threads. The first practice braid is best done with two strands of light-colored material and two strands of dark. Begin by anchoring the ends and holding the two dark strands in your right hand, the two light ones in your left. Take the outside (or far left) light strand, bring it under the other light strand, under the inner dark strand, up between the two dark strands, and back across the inner dark strand. What was originally the outside light thread has become the inner light thread (Figure 157).

Next, begin with the far right dark thread, which goes behind the inner dark thread, under the inner light thread, up between the two light strands, and back across the inner light strand. What was originally the outside dark thread has now become the inner dark thread. Repeat this, working alternately the far-right and far-left outside strands. The thread to be worked next is always the higher of the two outside threads.

Twisting the Fringe

The fringe on card weavings can be twisted in order to group colors, control the fringe, and create a full spiraling finish. Twisting is very simple, and requires only that groups of threads be twisted first in one direction, then together with another group in the opposite direction (Figure 159). This twist will hold, but should be bound at the bottom by wrapping, tying, or knotting to keep it secure and tight. The kind of yarn and the original twist of the threads will affect how the fringe twists.

Tying the Half Knot and the Square Knot

The half knot and the square knot give strong interest and sure control when knotted in rows to form warp end fringes. These knots both require four strands or groups of threads, and the half knot is essentially a repetition of just the first half of the square knot. The square knot, when tied in a series, forms a row of flat knots. The half knot creates a similar texture, but with a twist or spiral. In each knot only the two outside strands are worked. The two middle threads are inert and should be held taut as the knotting progresses (Figure 160).

Figure 156. (Above) The four-strand braid.

Figure 157. Detail of acrylic wall hanging, 4″ wide, by Hilda Rasmussen. The fringe at the top was twisted around a wire armature and held in place with wrapping.

Figure 158. Detail of wool cape woven by the author. The fringe was worked in four-strand braiding.

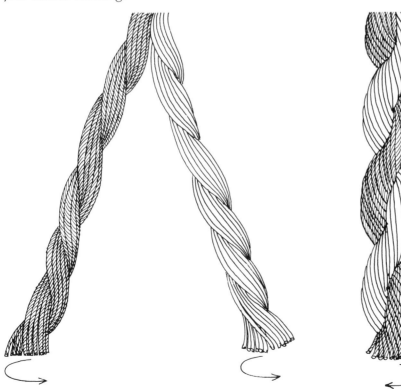

Figure 159. Twisting the fringe.

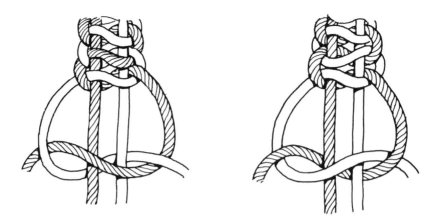

Figure 160. *The square knot and the half-knot.*

Figure 161. *Detail of a wool and jute hanging by Donna Armstrong. Both four-strand round braiding and rows of square knotting have been used for the fringe.*

To start knotting a row of half knots, align the four strands or threads parallel to one another, with the ends toward you. With the two middle threads away pulled toward you, place the right-hand strand over the top of the two middle threads, and under the left-hand thread. Take the left-hand strand under the two middle threads, and bring it up through the loop formed by the right-hand strand as shown in the illustration. Each knot in the series must be tied with the right-hand thread being worked first. For a reverse spiral, each knot in the series must begin with the left-hand thread worked first.

The half knot makes up the first half of the square knot; the right-hand thread goes over the middle two, and under the left-hand thread, which then goes under the two middle threads, and up through the loop formed by the right-hand strand. The second half of the square knot requires that you take the left-hand strand over the top of the two middle threads and under the right-hand strand, then take the right-hand strand under and up through the loop formed by the left-hand strand (see Figure 160). If you combine these two halves, you'll have a row of flat square knots.

Making Tassels

Tassels often add a pleasing fullness and finish to card weavings. Figure 163 shows how they can be used effectively as a fringe. Making tassels is easy and is clearly shown in Figure 162. Tassels can be simple or very complex, but basically a number of strands of an appropriate length are grouped together, tied in the middle, doubled over, and bound or wrapped into place. The tie that held the original strands together can serve as a means of attaching the tassel to the weaving or fringe.

Adding Beads

Beads, bells, and other objects can be sewn on where desired after the card weaving is finished, or they can be integrated into the piece as weaving progresses (Figures 165 and 166). Objects that are worked in during weaving are more a real part of the process, but pieces sewn on later can also enhance the look and feel of a card weaving. The beads are best worked in, as illustrated in Figure 164, on what is essentially a second weft thread, while the normal weft thread holds the warp threads tightly and securely in place. The beads are strung up, pushed along, and dropped into place where needed.

Making Fringe

Additional material can easily be "laid in" with the regular weft thread as a weaving progresses (Figures 167 and 168). There's no need to knot or tie the material being laid in, since the twisting of the warp threads and the tightness of the weave insure that the material laid in, whether fleece, yarn, raffia, or long feathers, will be held securely. Fringe can be inserted

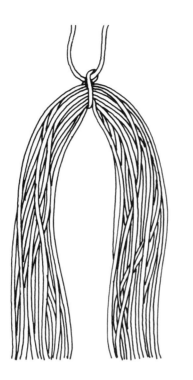

Figure 162. Making a tassel.

Figure 163. A hanging in plied goat hair, 4" wide, by the author. The tassels were made by the method illustrated in Figure 162 and attached to the weaving with a four-strand braid.

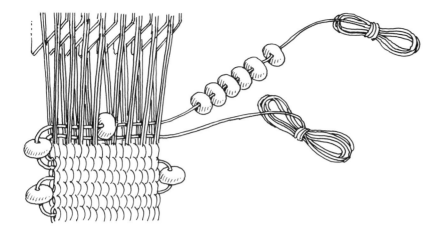

Figure 164. Adding beads during weaving.

Figure 165. Two wool bell-pulls, each 2½" wide, by Robert Cranford. The bells and beads were sewn on after the weaving was completed.

Figure 166. *A cotton band with flattened copper pennies, 1" wide, by the author. The pennies were worked into the weaving as illustrated in Figure 164.*

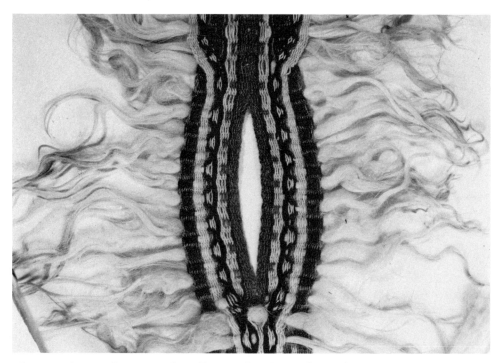

Figure 167. *Detail of a wool neckpiece, by the author. The fringe consists of long locks of natural sheep's wool laid in along with the weft thread during weaving.*

Figure 168. Two wool caps worked in sprang netting with card-woven straps by Jackie Wollenberg. During the card weaving, a thread was laid in with the regular weft thread to form long loops extending out on one side. Later this looped fringe was twisted and gathered to form a cap.

to extend out one side or both sides, or it can be pulled to the surface in the center of a weaving.

Decreasing Warp Threads

An interesting way of shaping card weavings is to decrease the number of warp threads as the weaving progresses (Figure 169). In this technique the warp threads to be decreased are cut near the anchoring knot, and the card or cards are slipped off. The threads are then laid through the open shed along with the normal weft thread. The decreased warp threads extend out in a group on the other side, where they can be trimmed or left as fringe. This manner of decreasing can be done evenly on both sides to bring the weaving to a symmetrical point (Figure 170). There are many ways of using this decreasing technique. For instance, warp threads may be decreased on only one side, from the center out, or irregularly.

Forming Card-woven Angles

Angles and curves of varying degrees are particularly useful for making handles and shaping trim for garments. A gentle curve is usually made by

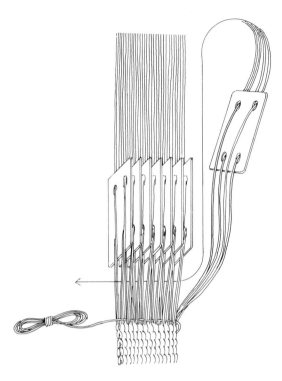

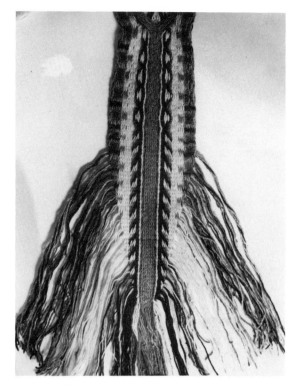

Figure 169. Decreasing warp threads.

Figure 170. Detail of a wool neckpiece, tapering from 8" to 1", by the author.

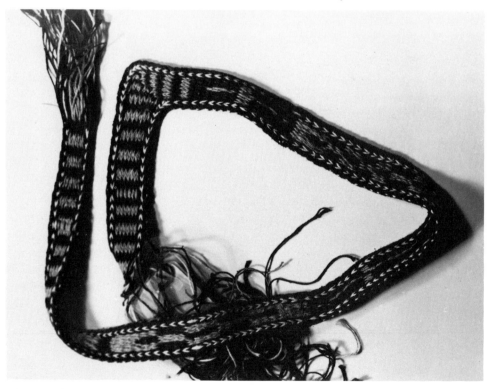

Figure 171. A cotton band, worked on 21 cards and shaped to form an angle, 2" wide, by Anne Blinks.

tightening warp tension on one side and loosening it on the other side during weaving. Angles and sharp curves are more involved (Figure 171). This technique takes practice for good results.

For a 45° angle to the left, weave to where the angle is to begin, then place the weft thread through the shed, but omit the threads that go through the 2 cards on the far left. Continue weaving, omitting the warp threads to the 2 left-hand cards each time, until the weaving comes to a point. This omitting of cards is always done on the side that will form the inside of the angle. Tension must now be adjusted so that the weaving can proceed in the new direction. One way to do this is to take a thin rod, a long nail, or a knitting needle, insert it along the newly created edge, and secure it in such a way as to bring both the rod and the new edge to a position at right angles to the warp threads as they're pulled from the anchor point toward the weaver. Continue weaving, picking up the warp threads gradually, until you are once again weaving full width. The degree and shape of the angle will depend on the number and frequency of cards dropped. The dropped cards shouldn't be turned as each new shed is formed. As dropped or omitted threads are brought back into the weaving after the angle has been made, the weaving card holes should be arranged in the proper order for the pattern being woven.

This technique can be learned only through experience, since the angle of the turn and the tension of the warp are difficult to control.

Sewing Strips Together

Card-woven bands can be sewn together and used very successfully as dress tops, capes, ponchos, vests, skirts, scarves, and rugs. Many wall hangings are made of several bands sewn together. Usually the most satisfactory technique for joining bands is to butt the edges to be stitched together, and with a tapestry needle and yarn similar to that used on the edges of the card weavings, whip-stitch the edges to one another. In whip-stitching, the needle goes through one edge to the other edge and back to the original edge so that the binding or sewing thread as it goes up the edge goes round and round catching both edges. Strips can also be crocheted together.

Figure 172. A wool bag made of 3½" strips, by Judith Kinnell. The fringe was tucked in under the lining.

Figure 173. A bag made from fine plied-wool yarn, 11" wide, by Robert Cranford.

Figure 174. The back of a contemporary cotton Tibetan bag, 14" wide, shown with the flap spread open. The bag was constructed of strips arranged both vertically and horizontally.

Figure 176. (Above) *A wool card-woven band applied down the center of a loom-woven cape by Robert Cranford.*

Figure 175. (Left) *A partially finished wool cape woven in strips by the author. Photograph by Bob Nugent.*

8. SOME SPECIAL APPROACHES

Figure 177. A card weaving using an inkle loom for tension. The heddle bar of the loom was removed to allow free passage of the warp threads. Tension is adjusted by loosening the wing nut and moving the tension bar. As the work progresses, the weaving is moved around on the loom, keeping the cards and weaving area where they can be worked most conveniently.

Figure 178. (Left) A flat card-loom arrangement with dowels and adjustable tension. Courtesy of the weaver, Kay Sekimachi.

Figure 179. (Right) A card-woven rug in progress, 34" wide, using a floor loom for tension.

Card weaving offers a wide range of possibilities for sculptural and dimensional effects. Most card weavings become belts of one sort or another but this chapter offers suggestions and information for the weaver whose interest goes beyond belt-making. The effects discussed can be used to create wall hangings and tapestries, but they may also be used in more functional card weavings.

Setting Up for Card Weaving

Three basic ways have been illustrated in previous chapters for creating tension in card weaving. Figure 6 shows a man working on a board with two pegs, Figure 40 shows one end of the weaving attached to a stationary object and the other end to the weaver's waist, and Figure 50 shows a weaving stretched between two stationary objects, in this case C-clamps. As weavings get wider and bulkier, something more is needed to maintain tension and to keep the weaving spread out. There are many ways to do this and for the most part it's a matter of imagination, what's available, and exactly what you want to weave. (Figures 177–179 show some ways of solving the problem).

A simpler means that involves less equipment is to tie the warp ends onto dowels as illustrated in Figures 181 and 182, and anchor the dowels wherever convenient. Any structure that will keep the cards and warp threads spread out and create tension should work.

Free-Form, or Open-Ended, Card Weaving

In the usual method of setting up a card weaving, the cards are pulled along the warp threads from the anchor point to the other end, which is tied to the waist. The warp threads are held parallel and under equal tension out in front of the weaver. Weaving is done by turning the cards and weaving between the body and the cards. In free-form card weaving, nearly the opposite happens. The cards aren't pulled the length of the warp to the far end. Instead, the weaving is carried on between the anchor point and the cards, with the cards working between the weaver and the weaving. The warp is combed as the weaving progresses and the weaver moves back, pulling the cards and controlling tension. In this method only one end of the warp is securely anchored (Figures 183 and 184).

This way of working is slow and the weaver must constantly deal with tension problems and loose ends, but it offers a number of interesting possibilities for shaping the weaving. Cards can easily be divided into groups that can be woven individually in different directions. The weaver can pull against the anchor point at different angles, causing the weaving to curve, spread, widen, and narrow. By working this way, warp threads from some cards can be drawn through the open shed to come out the other side so that warp becomes weft and weft becomes warp. Groups of threads and cards can literally be picked up and moved anywhere in the weaving. Warp threads can be held by the hand, tied to a belt, or wherever convenient, so

Figure 180. *A tubular linen card weaving by Kay Sekimachi, woven on the loom arrangement pictured in Figure 178.*

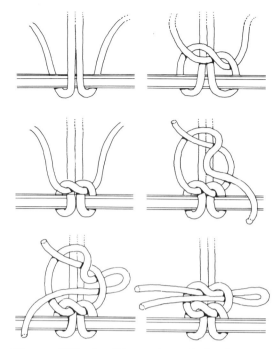

Figure 181. *An illustration of the knot used to tie warp ends onto a dowel.*

Figure 182. *A card weaving tied onto dowels.*

Figure 183. *A weaving of plastic coated wire in progress, by Dolores Levin.*

Figure 184. An open-ended weaving in progress using jute, wool, and rayon, by Diana Mitchell.

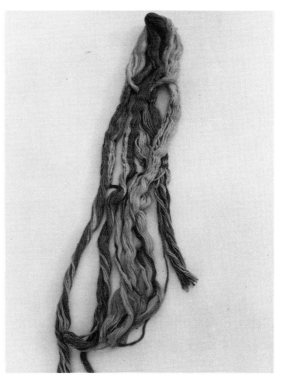

Figure 185. A cotton hanging where groups of threads were threaded through individual holes and then woven in a free-form manner.

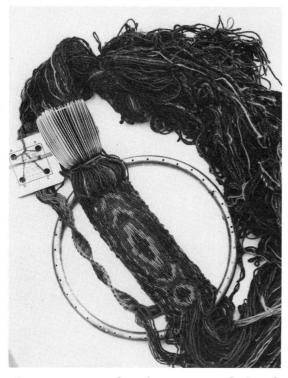

Figure 186. A wool card weaving worked with a 10″ metal hoop, by Linda Griggs.

Figure 187. A weaving in single-ply wool using 50 cards, by the author.

Figure 188. *A cotton hanging, 6" wide, by Patricia Campbell. In the beginning it was woven in two sections to form a slit.*

Figure 189. *A wool hanging, 7" wide, by Janet Bucknam. This piece was woven as a long, flat 5" band with slits. After weaving, the band was twisted and convoluted to form a dimensional hanging.*

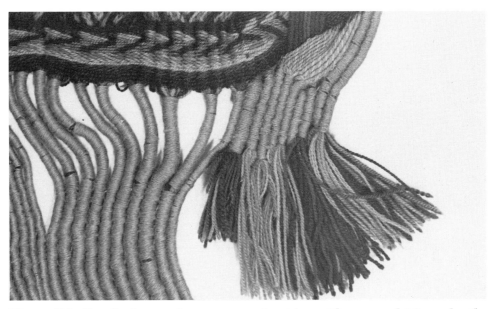

Figure 190. *Detail of a wool cape woven in strips with wrapped fringe, by the author.*

that the cards can be turned. Working on an armature or board as pictured in Figure 184 can be very helpful.

In free-form card weaving the cards act primarily as a simple shedding mechanism. Individual cards can be shifted and rearranged without destroying their ability to make a shed. The weave produced by cards is sturdy and dense, so that even open or loose areas have strength, stability, and the characteristic twists of card weaving.

Weaving Slits and Layers for Dimension

Slits, openings, and layers cause changes in the shape, texture, and design of weavings and add special interest to wall hangings. Slits and openings can be made vertically by using individual weft threads for weaving groups of warp threads. Figure 187 shows a slit being formed and Figures 188 and 189 show how they can function in weaving. Vertical openings in the warp can also be created by leaving sections of the warp unwoven.

A striking series of four-strand, tightly twisted cords can be created from the warp threads by turning the cards in one direction continuously without passing the weft thread through the shed. Each series of four strands from each card will produce one spiral.

Slits and openings offer possibilities for convoluting and winding bands together to form layers. Bands with openings can be woven on and added as needed to construct a larger dimensional piece. Layered weaving can be created in a number of ways, several of which are shown in the photographs in this chapter. One important means of producing slits, layers, and sculptural effects is the double weave, which is explained fully in Chapter 6.

Rearranging cards can be done at any time and can result in interesting surface texture and linear movement. Figure 191 shows how this is done. Sections of warp can be woven and then shifted during weaving so that one layer of weaving goes over another layer (Figure 192) or individual cards can be shifted so that warp threads are stretched across either on top of or underneath the weaving. Any number of cards may be involved in such a shift. Depending on the width of the piece, tension may have to be adjusted or warp threads retied to allow for the new position. If cards are moved frequently, puckered areas will appear, often with interesting rises and depressions in the weaving surface.

Varying the Warp Threads

Warp threads can be varied to add interest and texture, and different weights and types of yarn can be combined in one weaving. Many warp threads can be threaded through each hole so that a wide weaving may take only a few cards. This creates a bulky, heavy weaving which shows the texture of card weaving beautifully by greatly enlarging the design and each turn of the threads (Figures 194 and 195). This method of threading can be done evenly so that each hole has the same number of threads, or it can be done unevenly, putting different numbers of threads through each hole and even possibly leaving some holes totally unthreaded.

Weavings can be expanded by adding new warp threads by means of the half hitch (Figure 196) or by laying the new warp threads through an open shed (Figure 197).

By working the weft thread very loosely, warp threads can be spread out, leaving open spaces and shaped areas (Figure 198). The weft thread may also be pulled very tight to condense and pack the warp (Figure 199).

All of these techniques have many variations, and each will be different in the hands of different weavers.

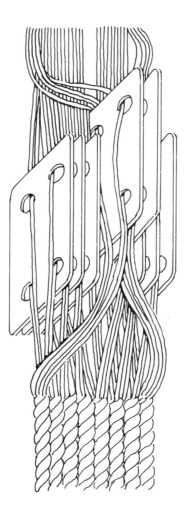

Figure 191. Cards are shifted laterally to move warp threads, create texture, and shift color. The cards to be shifted are actually picked up and moved to a new position, then tucked back into the pack of cards.

Figure 192. Detail of the back of a wool hanging, 34" wide, by Bettie Adams. It was woven as one piece using a loom for tension. Woven sections cross over and around to create layers and linear movement.

Figure 193. A hanging threaded in vertical stripes by the author. Cards have been shifted during weaving to create the braided effect.

Figure 194. Detail of a wool hanging, 7" wide, by Karen Myers. The weaving used 20 cards and many strands of plied yarn were threaded through each hole.

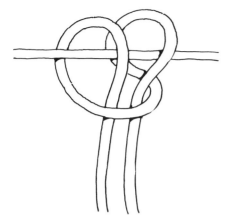

Figure 195. (Above) The half-hitch used for attaching new warp threads.

Figure 196. (Right) Detail of a wool hanging, 8″ wide, by Donna Armstrong. Part of the fringe was braided and part was re-threaded and woven in the original pattern, but with many threads going through each hole and using only a few cards.

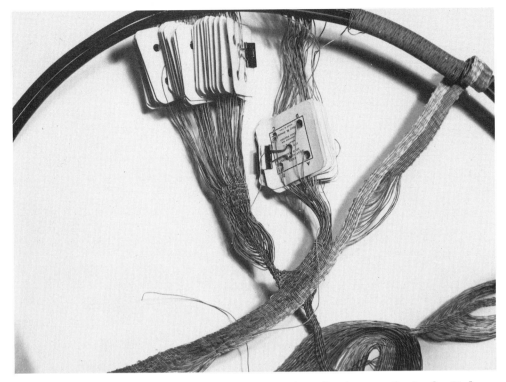

Figure 197. Detail of a weaving in progress using plastic coated wire by Dolores Levin. The direction of the warp threads has been changed by loosening and tightening tension. New warp threads have been added by looping through open sheds and then threading the strands through cards.

Figure 198. A cotton and wool hanging tapering from 8″ to 1½″, by Lillian Elliott. This piece was woven loosely to create an open meshwork.

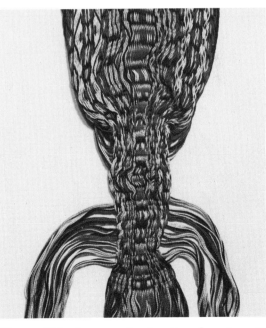

Figure 199. A mercerized cotton hanging, 8″ wide, by Patricia Campbell. The shaping was achieved by pulling weft threads.

GLOSSARY

Alternate Threading. A method of threading in which one card is threaded from the right, the next from the left, and so on.

Brocade. A raised design on the surface of the card weaving, usually created by floating weft threads.

Double-Face. A technique where the cards are turned continuously two turns away and two turns toward the weaver. Half the warp threads will show on the upper surface of the weaving, and half will show on the lower surface. A common weft thread binds the fabric.

Double Weave. A method of weaving two layers of fabric simultaneously.

Draft. *See* Pattern Draft.

Card Weaving. Tablet weaving in Britain.

Harness. The frame within the loom on which the heddles are hung. In Britain this is called a shaft.

Heddle. Heddles hold and guide warp threads on the loom. A weaving shed is formed when harnesses holding the heddles and warp threads are raised or lowered. The holes in card weaving can be compared to heddles.

Ikat. A weaving technique in which the warp or weft threads are bound and dyed before weaving.

Maniple. An ecclesiastical vestment.

Open-Ended Card Weaving. Card weaving in which the warp threads are anchored securely at just one end. The weaving develops between the anchor point and the cards, with the warp ends nearest the weaver left free.

Pattern. The design on the card-woven surface.

Pattern Draft. The graphed pattern that gives threading instructions for each card hole.

Paired Threading. *See* Alternate Threading.

Ply. Yarn strands are twisted together to form a single thread. The number of strands determines the number of plies.

Reed. A comblike structure for ordering and spacing warp threads on the loom. Used also to beat the weft thread into place.

Seine Twine (Seaming Twine). A strong, tightly spun cotton twine.

Shed. The open area between layers of warp threads through which the weft thread passes. In card weaving, each new shed is formed by a forward or backward rotation of the cards.

Shuttle. A tool that holds the weft thread and carries it through the shed. It can be used to beat the weft thread into place.

Skip-Hole Technique. A method of card weaving in which some card holes are left empty, causing depressions on the woven surface and allowing the weft thread to show.

Sprang. A netting technique where the interlinking of strands is achieved through twisting.

Spun in the Grease. Wool spun into yarn before scouring.

Tablet Weaving. Card weaving.

Tubular Card Weaving. A method for weaving a tube by using the weft thread to pull the two edges of a card weaving together.

Warp. The threads that go through the holes in the cards.

Weft. The thread that passes through each new shed and binds the warp threads together.

BIBLIOGRAPHY

Books

Atwater, M. M., *Byways in Handweaving*. New York: the Macmillan Co., 1954

————, *Notes on Card Weaving*, rev. & enl. New York: the Universal School of Handicrafts, 1944

————, *Shuttlecraft Course in Card Weaving*. Dittoed material, 75 drafts for card weaving.

Birrell, V., *The Textile Arts: A Handbook of Fabric Structure and Design Processes*. New York: Harper and Row, 1959

Branting, Agnes, and Lindblom, Andreas, *Medieval Embroideries and Textiles in Sweden*. Uppsala, 1932

Broholm, H. C., and Hald, M., *Costumes of the Bronze Age in Denmark*. Copenhagen, 1940

Clifford, L. I., *Card Weaving*. Peoria, Illinois: the Manual Arts Press, 1947

Emery, I., *The Primary Structure of Fabrics*. Washington, D.C.: The Textile Museum, 1966

Groff, R. E., *Card Weaving or Tablet Weaving*. McMinnville, Oregon: Robin and Russ Handweavers, after 1958

Hald, M., *Brikvaening*. Copenhagen: Byldendalske Boghandel-Nordisk Forlag, 1932

Lehmann-Filhes, M., *Ueber Brettchenweberei*. Berlin: Verlag Dietrich Reimer, 1901

Peach, M. W., *Tablet Weaving*. Leicester, England: Dryad Handicrafts, 1926

Pralle, H. *"Tablet Weaving," An Old Peasant Craft*. Leicester, England: Dryad Handicrafts, 1920

Roth, H. Ling, *Ancient Egyptian and Greek Looms*. Halifax, England: Bankfield Museum, 1951

Tablet Weaving. Leicester, England: the Dryad Press, in print

Van Gennep, A., and Jequier, G., *Le Tissage aux Cartons et son Utilisation Decoratif dans l'Egypte Ancienne*. Neuchatel, Switzerland: Delachaux & Niestle, 1916

Articles

Atwater, M. M., "Cardweaving." *Handicrafter,* May–June: 9–13, 1931

———, "Egyptian Cardweaving is a Fascinating Little Craft You Will Enjoy." *Modern Priscilla,* September, 1924

———, "Stunting on the Cards." *The Weaver,* 2:25–30, 1937

Choquette, A., "Cardweaving." *The Tie-Up* (published by the Southern California Handweavers Guild), November, 1972

Collingwood, P., "A Shaped Tie Woven With Tablets." *Quarterly of the Association of Weavers, Spinners and Dyers* (England), 44:435–436, 1962

Crockett, C., "Considering Cardweaving." *Handweaver and Craftsman,* Summer, 1971

Crowfoot, G. M., "The Tablet-woven Braids from the Vestments of St. Cuthbert at Durham." *The Antiquaries Journal,* 19:1, 1939

Glanz, M., "Cardweaving." *The Tie-Up,* June, 1970

Hartnett, F. and Russell, E., "Transposing a Card Weaving Pattern to a Pattern for a 4-Harness Loom." *The Tie-Up,* October, 1970

Henshall, A., "Five Tablet-woven Seal Tags." *Archaeological J.* (England), CXXI: 154–162, 1964

Lambert, A., "Methods of Peasant Textile Work." *Ciba Review,* 2403–2404

Schuette, M., "Tablet Weaving." *Ciba Review,* No. 117, 1956

Seagroat, M., "A Weaving Mystery, or, New Light on an Old Girdle." *Quarterly of the Association of Weavers, Spinners and Dyers,* 50: 626–8, 1964

Staudigel, O., "Tablet Weaving." *Quarterly of the Association of Weavers, Spinners and Dyers* (England), 38: 257–261, 1961

Youse, C. M., "Card Weaving Technique." *The Weaver,* Jan–Feb: 26–28, 1941

Magazines

Crafts, published by the Crafts Advisory Committee, 28 Haymarket, London SW1Y 4SU, England

Handweaver and Craftsman, 220 Fifth Avenue, New York, New York 10001

Quarterly Journal of the Association of Weavers, Spinners, and Dyers, available from Miss Ruth Hurle, 47 East Street, Saffron Waldon, Essex, England

Shuttle, Spindle, and Dyepot, 1013 Farmington Avenue, West Hartford, Connecticut 06101

SUPPLIERS LIST

Berga/Ullman
P.O. Box 831
1 Westerly Road
Ossining, New York 10562
Weaving yarns

Briggs and Little's Woolen Mill, Ltd.
York Mills, Harvey Station
New Brunswick, Canada
Weaving yarns

The J. and H. Clasgens Co.
New Richmond, Ohio 45157
Weaving yarns

Condon and Sons Ltd.
Charlottetown
P.E. Island, Canada
Wool weaving yarns

Coulter Studios
138 East 60th Street
New York, New York 10022
Rya rug yarns

Craft Yarns
603 Mineral Spring Ave.
Pantucket, Rhode Island 02862
Weaving yarns

Creative Handweavers
3824 Sunset Blvd.
Los Angeles, California 90026
Cards and weaving yarns

Dharma Trading Company
Box 1288
Berkeley, California 95704
Cards and weaving yarns

K. R. Drummond
30 Hart Grove
London W.5.
Art and craft books, cards—by appointment only

Dryad
Northgates
Leicester Le14QR, England
Equipment, yarns, dyes

Everyday Handweavers
5300 Soquel Drive
Soquel, California

Frederick J. Fawcett, Inc.
129 South St.
Boston, Massachusetts 02111
Weaving yarns, good selection of cords and linen

Folklorico
P.O. Box 625
Palo Alto, California 94302
Cards and weaving yarns

Fort Crailo Yarns Co.
2 Green St. Dept. 4
Rensselaer, New York 12144
Wool weaving yarns

A. K. Graupner
Corner House,
Valley Road,
Bradford 1
Yorks, England
Yarns

William Hall & Co.
177 Stanley Road
Cheadle Hulme,
Cheshire
Cotton yarns

The Handweaver
111 East Napa St.
Sonoma, California 95476
Cards and weaving yarns, good selection of mill ends

The Handweavers Studio and Gallery
29 Haroldstone Road
London E.17
Weaving equipment, cards, yarns, tuition and information

Frank Horring & Sons
27 High West Street
Dorchester, Dorset
Weaving equipment

Lily Mills, Co.
Dept. HWH
Shelby, North Carolina 28150
Weaving yarns, good selection of cotton yarns

Macramé and Weaving Supplies
63 E. Adams St.
Chicago, Illinois 60603
Weaving yarns

The Makings
1916 University Ave.
Berkeley, California 95704
Cards and weaving yarns

The Mannings
R.D. East Berlin
Pennsylvania 17316
Weaving yarns

Multiple Fabric
Dudley Hill
Bradford 4, England
Horsehair yarn and tightly spun mohair, wool and camel hair in natural colors

Natural Craft
2199 Bancroft Way
Berkeley, California
Square, triangular, and hexagonal cards, and weaving yarns

Robin and Russ
533 North Adams St.
McMinnville, Oregon 97128
Cards and weaving yarns

School Products Company, Inc.
312 East 23rd Street
New York, New York 10010
Card loom, cards, and weaving yarns

"Some Place"
2990 Adeline St.
Berkeley, California 94703
Card loom, plastic cards, and weaving yarns

Tahki Imports
336 West End Avenue
New York, New York 10023
Greek and Irish yarns

Wild and Woolly Weaving
12 South 15th St. Suite 201
San Jose, California 95112
Cards, can be purchased in bulk, and weaving yarns

The Woolgatherer
47 State Street
Brooklyn Heights, New York 11201
Weaving yarns

The Yarn Depot
545 Sutter St.
San Francisco, California 94102
Cards in normal and heavy weight and weaving yarns

INDEX